"Kelly Oxford's writing is hila........ ....dass
Canadian sister I never had." —Mindy Kaling

"I have worshipped the mind of Kelly Oxford for eons. I love the way
she synthesizes the crazy stew of bad decision-making, rage, panic,
anxiety, and total euphoria, often all in the same day. Kelly Oxford's
concise, whip-smart observations feel eerily universal. *When You
Find Out the World Is Against You* shows that there is something to be
learned from even the most absurd or devastating moments of life."
—Jill Soloway

"Kelly is part geek, part freak. *When You Find Out the World Is Against
You* shows us ourselves: our sensitivities, our awkward moments, our
strange desires. She takes us through summer camp, dating, rape
culture, Trump, death. . . . Kelly Oxford c'est moi."
—James Franco

"Two things I'm grateful for: how imperfect Kelly Oxford is at life
and decision-making, and how terrific she is at writing about what a
goddamn mess she is." —Patton Oswalt

"Kelly Oxford is a beautiful writer. She finds beauty in the mundane
and humor in everyday eccentricities. She is our present-day, funny
Joan Didion." —Gia Coppola

"With her signature wit . . . [Oxford] delves into the ups and downs
of this thing we call life." —*Cosmopolitan*

"Bitingly funny." —*Glamour*

"Darkly hilarious essays." —*InStyle*

"Fantastically funny." —*Global News*

"*When You Find Out the World Is Against You* is Kelly at her honest and most disarmingly funny best. Filled with biting, wise, and laugh-out-loud insights, this vastly entertaining collection of vignettes will make you think as much as it will make you laugh." —49th Shelf

"[Oxford] draws on her strengths of both emotional and tangible memory to paint her scenes. Oxford shares not by over-sharing, but by being honest about what she has felt or feels. . . . Oxford's tone has the air of a one on one conversation, rather than that of a person bellowing one-liners into the worldwide abyss." —Vue Weekly

"Oxford's new book, *When You Find Out the World Is Against You*, is an extension of her social media brand (clever, insightful, self-deprecating). . . . She once again bares it all in a series of nostalgia-inducing personal essays, some LOL funny . . . and others poignant." —*Fashion*

"Funny, sharp and unique." —*Globe and Mail* (UK)

"The essays in *When You Find Out the World Is Against You* pack a straight-up emotional punch." —*Châtelaine*

"[Oxford's] 12 essays—about growing up, marriage and parenting, etc. etc.—are clever and unfailingly amusing. The girl can turn a phrase." —*The Star* (Toronto)

WHEN YOU
FIND OUT
THE WORLD
IS AGAINST

YOU

ALSO BY KELLY OXFORD

Everything Is Perfect When You're a Liar

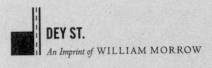

DEY ST.
An Imprint of WILLIAM MORROW

WHEN YOU
FIND OUT
THE WORLD
IS AGAINST
YOU

**AND OTHER
FUNNY MEMORIES
ABOUT AWFUL
MOMENTS**

KELLY OXFORD

To McDonald's and Oprah

DEY ST.

The names of certain individuals have been changed to protect their privacy.

WHEN YOU FIND OUT THE WORLD IS AGAINST YOU. Copyright © 2017 by Kelly Oxford. All rights reserved. Printed in the United States of America. No part of this book may be used or reproduced in any manner whatsoever without written permission except in the case of brief quotations embodied in critical articles and reviews. For information, address HarperCollins Publishers, 195 Broadway, New York, NY 10007.

HarperCollins books may be purchased for educational, business, or sales promotional use. For information, please email the Special Markets Department at SPsales@harpercollins.com.

A hardcover edition of this book was published in 2017 by Dey Street Books, an imprint of William Morrow.

FIRST DEY STREET BOOKS PAPERBACK EDITION PUBLISHED 2018.

Designed by Paula Russell Szafranski

Library of Congress Cataloging-in-Publication Data has been applied for.

ISBN 978-0-06-232278-4

18 19 20 21 22 DIX/LSC 10 9 8 7 6 5 4 3 2 1

CONTENTS

A BRIEF INTRODUCTION

This is a book for anyone who has ever felt like the world is against them. In other words, this is a book for everyone. Glad you are here.

Never Play Piggy

"Mom, this is my last chance."

From her lounger on the deck of our cabin, Mom fluttered her lids, like she might break focus from her true loves, Margaret Atwood and gin and tonic, and look at me—her daughter—but she didn't.

"I'm eleven, it's already 1988. I'm getting boobs. I *have* to go to summer camp this year. I should have already gone to camp." In my "camp fantasy" I meet a boy who thinks

I'm very funny and likes me a lot. Due to my underdeveloped body, the camp counselor has no suspicions that I am a horny teen and am able to sneak away with the boy and kiss him all summer long. If I have boobs at camp: 1.) A boy may like me for my boobs and 2.) It will be harder for me to hide that puberty has me amped up!

She sipped, laughed, and replied, "Remember you told me you had a lump and made me take you to the doctor because you thought it was cancer, but really it was your breast growing?"

Of course she would ridicule my concerns about cancer at a time like this. I swatted away my mortal enemy, a mosquito . . . all this suffering (the heat, mosquitoes, my emotional anguish regarding a rite of passage I was going to miss!) and she lay there drinking and laughing about my cancer boob.

"Mom! I'm serious. I want to go to camp while I'm still young, before I really get boobs. You want a naïve girl with boobs away at camp?"

With that, she looked up at me. "Let me think about it. Can you go inside and make some orange juice?"

I was angry that she was avoiding the camp talk, but replied, "Yes, of course." Because I knew that in order to go to summer camp I would probably have to: 1.) do everything she wanted me to do, or 2.) manipulate this situation via her guilt over denying her helpful child the one thing she wanted most.

I stood up and waddled across the hot deck on the sides

of my scalding feet. My new boobs shook ever so slightly as I walked. I hadn't been joking about wanting to go to camp before I got boobs. I liked talking to boys; talking to boys while away at camp was a key factor in all of my camp fantasies. I couldn't even imagine what it would be like with boobs in the way. And I knew my hormones were really kicking in because I was sweating through my shirts all the time and I kept rereading my Judy Blumes.

I'd already had my first eruption of acne, which I had worn with extreme pride as it signified my impending teendom.

"Do you have chicken pox?" my eleven-year-old friends had asked.

"No!" I had boasted, "It's acne, can you believe it, I'm only eleven!" (Side note: Had my dermatologist told me that at the age of thirty-seven I'd still be applying cream to my face every night in my battle with acne, I might have ended it all at that point.)

My mother looked forward to summer vacation almost as much as my little sister, Lauren, and I did. Most summers she was not working and my dad would stay home in Edmonton while Mom, Lauren, and I would pack up the old Volvo station wagon and go to the lake cabin for two months. I felt like another person when I was at the cabin, in the middle of nowhere.

Mom and I spent our summers the same way, reading books. She would do it in the sun, tucking her thick, black hair behind the bows of her sunglasses and leaning back into the plastic chairs, basting herself in layers of Johnson & Johnson's baby oil. She would spend weeks inviting more and more potential melanoma onto her body while sipping a gin and tonic. I would read inside the house, away from the bugs and smells and cancer, and was only allowed to take the occasional sip of gin, but didn't see that as a privilege. That stuff tasted like pain. Lauren, well, I didn't really know what Lauren did. She was two years younger than me and didn't like reading, but she also didn't hang out with me. We were rarely within fifty feet of each other except when we were watching *Three's Company* in the afternoon or sleeping, after Lauren returned from the woods or the beach, wherever she was, rinsed the day down the shower drain, and climbed into the bunk above mine.

I loved nothing more than spending two months lying in bed, with my stack of fifty new books from Greenwoods' Bookshoppe (RIP Greenwoods' Bookshoppe) on my dresser, the soles of my feet planted firmly above me on the rough cedar walls of our bedroom.

Summers were for books, cabin bunk beds, Casey Kasem on the radio, investigating septic fields, and watching the rural television stations caught by crooked tinfoil-covered antennae on top of our old TV. These were the things I was allowed to do, and I was totally content doing them until I discovered that I was missing something very important that many of my best friends (the characters in the books I was devouring) were experiencing . . . summer camp.

I'd recently read a terribly written old soapy series book

where two sisters went to camp. The less pretty, bookworm sister was not suspected as a horndog, while the pretty cheerleader sister was. Counselors always had an eye on the sister with the B cups while the flat-as-a-board sister was allowed free rein as a kissing bandit. This was the fantasy. Another book that I loved was about a boy named Rudy, who hated camp and tried to escape; it was called *I Want to Go Home!* I figured my camp experience would be one or the other. If I couldn't find a guy, I would escape. Either way—summer adventure.

In the humid, shadowy air of our small cabin kitchen, several flies flew around my face and into my eyes. My mom came to the screen door and I pounced, because clearly Mom had, in the forty-five seconds she had been alone, come to a decision about this enormously important, life-changing question.

"Did you think about it?" I asked, shooing the flies away with one hand and holding the frozen container of orange juice concentrate with the other.

"Mom! I'm dead serious!" My hand was now nearly frozen to the black-and-orange tube.

"It isn't your last chance," Mom said, pulling her sunglasses forward and letting her thick hair fall, as she held the screen door open far too nonchalantly, allowing more disease-infested flies to enter the kitchen.

The reality was that for over a year I'd been pushing to go to camp. Not even the whole summer at camp, just a week (we weren't the Rockefellers).

"It really is my last chance, Mom. I'm being very honest

with you because I need you to know how bad I want to go to camp! Please, it's just for a week."

"I'll think about it."

Mom saying "I'll think about it," felt like the vibrations on my hands when a fish nibbled the cheese bait at the end of my fishing line. She was buying it. "Mom! It's already August!! There is no time to think!" She kept walking, but waved her hand back at me, which was her signal that she had heard me.

Tiny hands twitching with excitement, I pulled the white plastic ring around and off the frozen juice cylinder. Making frozen juice was so weird. The containers felt industrial, like I was a robot performing some huge service. I was turning a trapped can of frozen juice into a pitcher of drinkable vitamins. I popped the metal part off the top and squeezed the frozen orange goop into a pitcher. That part always reminded me of taking a poo.

"It's probably too late, you know, to get to camp this year." Lauren sat at the long Formica-yellow and chrome kitchen table, swinging her feet under it.

"Oh my God." I groaned. When the hell did she show up?

Lauren was playing Tetris on our new Game Boy, which we shared (as I mentioned, we weren't the Rockefellers). "I want some of that juice," she said, not looking up from her falling pieces.

"Get it yourself! PS, I get the Game Boy at two o'clock." With the wooden spoon I stabbed at the frozen orange block.

"I hope Mom lets you go to camp." She exhaled, and

looked up at me with her enviable blue eyes. My eyes are hazel but everyone in my family called them brown. My dad would say to me, "You're so full of shit your eyes are brown," which I think was 1.) inappropriate, and 2.) something perhaps his father had lovingly told him once, since my eyes were identical to his and men of their generations were awful at showing emotions like love or gratitude for having a lovely daughter with hazel eyes.

"If you go to camp this year, I'll get to go next year, way before you ever got to go. And I'll get Tetris to myself while you are gone," Lauren gloated.

She was right. The first kid has to wait forever to try something or get something new, a Walkman, a Game Boy, camp . . . it's the bane of every eldest child's existence. Fighting to get your bedtime extended to a later hour, arguing over how many pairs of ruffle socks you're allowed to wear to school. The second child does not have to do any crusading. Nothing. Entitled and lazy assholes, all of them.

I put the plastic pitcher down into the sink, turned on the hot water, and poured scalding water over the frozen juice. Then I stopped and chopped up the frozen juice, added a bit more water, and chopped some more. When it was finally melted I grabbed an ice cube tray out of the freezer, cracked the whole tray out, and filled the rest of the jug with cold water and ice cubes. There. Done.

"Kelly, remember the time we found a hyperventilating duck in the basement?" my sister asked, still staring at the new Game Boy. I stared back at her with a dead look on my face, hoping she would look up, even for a moment, and feel how little I liked her right then.

We shared this cabin with my Aunt Susan, Uncle Earle, my cousins, and Gram. Sometimes we were all at the cabin and sometimes we weren't. The basement was weird, well lit, and enormous. Concrete, with walls framed, inexplicably, with old, white cardboard. The cardboard walls let us play like mice, peeling up a corner of a wall to sneak into another room. But one day, as we slipped from one room to another, chasing each other through the cardboard walls, we stumbled upon a duck, just sitting in the far corner of the back room and hyperventilating. Uncle Earle came downstairs and stood, stunned, repeating, "There is a hyperventilating duck in the basement." My parents, Aunt Susan, and Gram all came down the basement stairs of the cabin to see, sure enough, there was a wood duck sitting on the floor, breathing very heavily. It was the only time my entire family would be in a basement together. We carried the duck outside and he flew away. The mystery of the duck in the basement was never solved. It seems rather poignant.

"Yeah. What about the duck?" I asked, squinting my eyes and praying she would look at me. I was sure I was seething annoyance—I could win an Oscar for this.

"Nothing. I was just thinking about it." She looked up and saw my face. She smiled and looked back down at her Game Boy, smugly knowing she would reap all the camp work I would accomplish myself.

"Your stupid orange juice is on the counter."

I opened the screen door without allowing flies to get

into the house because I care about sanitation. I stepped out onto the patio that surrounded the A-frame cabin perched on a small hill, in between poplar and birch trees, above a little beachfront grass and sand.

Every year my dad would paint the deck chocolate-brown and every year it would peel in the spots where the sun broke through the trees and landed. Under the summer sun, the dark paint burned the shit out of my feet.

"Mom, I need to go to camp. I'm bored and I hate my sister. You gave me a dud."

"Go play with Stephanie, she's here this week." Stephanie was my summer "lake friend" who lived in the same bay. I'd visit her a few times a year in the city, but we spent almost every day in the summer together at the lake.

"But Stephanie is going to camp!" (I lied.)

"Did you finish the orange juice?" My mom picked up her gin and tonic and the ice clinked.

"Yes, does that mean I can go to camp?"

"No."

I wondered how many other useless tasks I'd be assigned before she felt I was worthy of camp. "Fine. I'm going to Stephanie's to see if she's still there, but I'm pretty sure she went to Camp Chapawee because she's the middle kid and her older sister did all the work for her!"

Walking to Stephanie's cabin was one of my favorite things to do at the lake. I took small, gamelike trails that had been swathed through the woods to connect the houses, and loops of gravel roads off the main one and down toward the lakefront.

There was nothing on the trail but bushes and dogs and wild raspberries. I'd never even seen another person on the trail. In the city I felt like I had to be constantly wary about every little thing. Once, a guy in an old rusted Datsun pulled up to us and asked us if we had seen his lost puppy and I screamed, "I READ ABOUT THIS KIDNAPPER'S TRICK! GET OUT OF HERE!" He drove off. Here, in the woods, I was free. Never anticipating abduction. There was one time when the people in the house off the trail invited us into their cabin to see their newborn kittens, and of course we went in. Later, my mother screamed at Lauren and me for entering their house to see those kittens. I realized I'd fallen for the "lost puppy" style of trick and swore never again to listen to strangers, even when they dangled the carrot of small animals.

But nothing terrible could ever happen in Harvest Moon Bay! The worst thing that could happen here would come at the hands of your own mother, depriving you of your destiny at Camp Chapawee.

The dogs by Stephanie's house—Irish setter sisters named Molly and Kelly—barked when they heard me stumbling out of the bushes. Their red color was lovely but they didn't seem like real dogs and I was kind of embarrassed that there was a dog in the village named Kelly. I hadn't told anyone that because so far no one had put two and two together. I was also oddly embarrassed that they were Irish setters and their owners had given them the Irish names. But ultimately, that was their cross to bear. Not mine.

Stephanie had an older sister, Esther, who was always

on the computer playing Jeopardy! when I visited her in the city and must have been lost without it at the cabin. She sat on the steps in her cutoffs and striped shirt, swatting mosquitoes away. "Is Stephanie home?" I asked. Esther looked up from her reading, expressionless, and then looked back down at her *Scientific American* magazine, calling, "Stephanie!"

I felt a sting and slapped my leg on instinct. Mosquitoes. There was a cloud of them around my legs. "Esther, I need to go inside. Can I go inside? I'm allergic to mosquitoes."

Esther didn't look up. "That's impossible. No one is allergic to mosquitoes."

"I am, I get huge welts. You're wrong. Can I please pass?" I realized, as I squeezed by, her arms motioning an "after you" sweeping gesture to match her rolling eyes, that I was getting the older-sister treatment I had been serving my sister earlier. I brushed more bloodsucking bugs from my legs as I climbed the steps and opened the door to Stephanie's cabin and instantly inhaled that "other family" smell. Always a combination of a family's most-often-cooked foods, their pets (if any), and their brand of laundry detergent. I considered Stephanie's family smell good because it was much like ours—dogless, Tide detergent, a hint of macaroni and cheese.

Stephanie was twelve days older than I was, also wore glasses, and had reddish blond hair, which was curly like mine, but it may have been a perm. I had never asked because I would just get jealous if it was a perm. I *really* wanted a perm (mostly just to experience what I'd seen women go through in movies like *Steel Magnolias*), but my (brown) hair was naturally wavy, and whenever I'd asked my mom for a perm she had told me it was unnecessary.

"Hey!" Stephanie said. She was always much more cheerful than I was, or else maybe her smile was just better.

"Can I use your DEET?" I held up the can. "I'm allergic to mosquitoes and they are everywhere out there."

"I don't care," she said.

I went outside to spray myself down because I was polite and didn't want to fill their okay-smelling house with DEET. Stephanie followed me. "You want me to spray you down?" I offered, finger on the trigger, can pointed at her legs.

"I'm good, they don't like me."

"Ugh!" I moaned. "Everyone I know says that! I'll come home with a hundred welts and no one else will have a bite. It isn't fair. My dad says mosquitoes are attracted to me because I'm sweet, but I know it isn't that! I'm not really that sweet!" I finished spraying my legs, realizing I was talking too much and that Stephanie had no idea why I was there. I was feeling the sting of the spray on the old bites that I'd now scratched raw.

"Esther gets bites, too," she said.

I looked over at Esther, and she had bugs all around her. I put the can of spray down beside her, on the deck. She looked up and I raised my eyebrows and gently tapped the top of the can. "You should really protect yourself, girl."

I turned to Stephanie. "I have a plan."

We walked down the road, passing Molly and Kelly, now

sleeping, toward the beach. We skirted the trees on someone's property, through the mushy grass and onto the sand as I told her about all the possibilities that awaited us at Camp Chapawee. "It's mixed, Stephanie. Girls and boys. Look at it!" I pointed down the bay. We could hear and see the camp kids playing in the water. Screaming, laughing. "That's where we need to be next week."

Stephanie tilted her freckled face up away from the sun. (I envied her freckles, too.) "Why, what's happening next week?"

"I mean, nothing in particular. I just want to go before I start middle school. Maybe I could make out with a boy."

Stephanie nodded. "I get it. We need some experience before middle school."

This was why I loved her. "Exactly. I want to have things to talk about when I start junior high school. I need some drama, some experience."

We both looked into the distance at the camp kids, as small as poppy seeds but far less benign than those little devils. "I mean, those kids are getting into trouble."

Stephanie nodded. "I don't know if it's that much fun. Esther didn't tell me much about it."

"Esther went!? I'm sure she won't tell me anything, but I bet it was amazing. Stephanie, we have to go." I was going for the hard sell. "It's like how all the great stories are about orphans because all the really great stuff can only happen to kids when their parents aren't around. Like sneaking off with boys! You think your parents will let you go?"

"For sure. My mom already asked me if I wanted to go."

Ugh, second children. Those bastards.

"Okay, good. Because I already told my mom you were going, you know, if she asks."

"We could go tomorrow," Stephanie said, with the casualness only a second child could ever possess. "It's Monday. New camp week."

I rushed home so fast that even my old neighbor dog, Lucy, lifted her head to see what the commotion was as I passed. I skirted our septic field (I generally passed this quickly, to be fair), crossed the yard, and passed the rhubarb patch and the umbrella-shaped clothing line. I stormed up the steps to the deck, ready to take on the world. "The world" was my mother, who controlled my eleven-year-old life. I think if you're a lucky kid, your mother controls your life. It sounds crazy, but it's true. Some parents didn't care, like Howie Turner's. He crapped his pants at school and his mom was a stay-at-home mom and didn't show up immediately with a new pair of pants. That was awful.

I'd adequately pumped myself up on this run home, not even thinking about mosquitoes or dogs. I was going to get her to say yes to camp. I was not going to let her change the subject. I would lay the guilt on thick if she didn't bite. I would tell her Stephanie was going tomorrow. I would not waver. I would not let her talk about anything else until she said yes.

I turned the corner and saw Mom and Lauren, clad in bathing suits and slathered in baby oil, in their lounge chairs, both eating chocolate-dipped Revello ice cream bars.

"Wait!" My focus was broken. "We had ice cream bars?"

"Yeah, in the freezer," Lauren said, crunching into the chocolate shell.

"Oh no!" Focus, damnit Kelly, focus. "Mom, I want to go to Camp Chapawee. Tomorrow. Stephanie is going and—"

"Yes, I already talked to her mom and called the camp. Go pack."

"Really?!" The ice cream bars were already a distant memory. "I'm going to camp?"

"Yes! Beside the phone is a list of things to pack. I had mini shampoos in the linen closet from our last camping trip. I put those on your bed. And the small duffel."

"And my cute sleeping bag? The pink one?"

"No, that's in Edmonton. Use the green one. It's in there, too." She paused, then turned to me.

"Kelly? You smell so much like bug spray. I know you hate mosquitoes—"

"Um, I'm allergic to them."

"—but that stuff isn't good for you. DEET causes tumors in animals."

"Fine." I wanted to say something about her slathering herself in baby oil, laughing in the face of cancer and UV damage, but I had just gotten a ticket to ride out of here in the morning.

"I'm going to have ice cream. And orange juice. Maybe the other way around. Then pack. Thanks."

"We drank all the orange juice," Lauren said. Of course they did.

· · ·

IT WAS A THREE-MINUTE drive on the dusty gravel road from our cabin on Robin Close, on the outer curve of the bay, across the range road, and into Camp Chapawee.

As we pulled up in my mom's gold Volvo station wagon, I saw a camp sign that wasn't visible from the range road. Twenty feet tall and crudely carved into large logs that hung above the road, it read, "Camp Chapawee Church Camp."

I was shocked, "Mom, it's a *church* camp!?"

We didn't go to church. I mean, we had for a bit. My mom had had some sort of an *issue with life* a couple of years before, and whatever that issue was resulted in our entire family having to go to church for a year. Like, out of nowhere. She had us confirmed and baptized and everything. Then we abruptly stopped going, I think because I complained a lot. I wasn't against the church itself—it was sort of fun to laugh about and two of the cute boys from my school were there—but it was really not something I wanted to do on a Sunday. If Sundays were truly God's day, God wouldn't have put those two boys in front of me at church, totally unkissable.

"Do you think we're going to have to do a ton of God activities? Does a preacher run this camp? Oh, man! This place was supposed to be mixed girls and boys! Are there going to be no boys?!" All of my hopes for this camp to be fun and amazing were very quickly going up in religious flames. I mean, the camp counselors might not know, but *God* knows you're horny before you get your boobs! Panic was setting in.

"They assured me it's pretty casual. Prayers at meals, that sort of thing." My mom seemed pleased at this revelation.

"Did you only bring me here because it's *church* camp?"

Mom smiled. "I didn't realize it was church camp either, Kelly."

Damn her.

Mom stopped the car beside a field where all the kids were being dropped off. I looked into the crowd. "I don't see Stephanie."

"I'm sure she's around." My mom placed her hand on the back of the passenger headrest and turned to me in the backseat. "You have everything?"

I nodded. "Yeah, but Stephanie isn't here." Did she want me to get out of the car into the sea of stranger kids without Stephanie?

"She's around, I'm sure. Go!"

I pushed open the Volvo door, which was wildly heavy for no reason (my stupid tiny hands!), and stepped into the dandelion-filled field.

The west edge of the field was dotted with a dozen small, wooden cabins. On the east side of the field were the dining hall and the lake. It seemed very simple; I supposed Jesus never needed much. I looked around at the kids in the field. I recognized no one. Everyone seemed to have come with someone. They were standing in groups as though they were all old friends, and here I was, the barely developed loner, looking for drama.

I walked into a group of maybe thirty or forty other kids, looking for Stephanie. "Hey!" I smiled at a girl who also wore large glasses, so I figured she suffered the same pain as I did—broken eyes. "I love your glasses," I said, with the sort of tone reserved for people you already know.

She smiled and said, "Thanks!" but it was a confused smile, and then she walked off. Rude.

I moved deeper into the crowd, toward where some boys were laughing really hard. They looked old. They looked old-enough-to-have-pubic-hair old, and I suddenly felt my boobs again as I walked. My boobs weren't big enough for a real bra yet, but they were too obvious to not wear one. I adjusted the strap on the cotton bathing suit top I'd started wearing. It looked sporty and kept me modest.

One of the guys was either Greek or hormonally advanced. He had hair growing all over his face and neck and under his thin yellow T-shirt with a drunk yellow and round "smiley face" on it.

I stopped near him and made brief eye contact. He laughed, bravely showing everyone his yellowed niblet teeth.

"Is this toddler camp?" He even pointed! Right at me!

I froze, and half laughed. "Yeah!" I breathed, "Toddlers! Good one! I just have very small hands, but the rest of my body is normal." I wondered if my bra was too restricting and looked at his friends for some sort of backup. They were all uninterested and chuckling, except for one boy, and lucky for me, he was the only cute boy out of all of them. Tan and tall, cute boy had a shaved head and giant round green eyes. He smiled a little at me, and shook his head, as an apology for the hairy guy with niblet teeth.

"Don't worry about him," he casually whispered to me, but I heard "I am in love with you, Kelly Oxford."

He patted my back, trying to be reassuring, but a little too hard. "He doesn't know how to act around girls." He winked. I heard "Be the mother of all my children. I only have round green eyes and tan skin to attract you. Did you know I came to summer camp to meet you and make your camp fantasies come true? I love you, Kelly Oxford."

My stomach dropped, my eyes welled with emotion. Tears were one of my true weaknesses in times of emotion. My body betrayals. If something is especially good or especially bad, my eyes always well up with tears. I'd been here for two minutes and I'd met the guy I'd be kissing all week. Summer camp was already the best decision I'd ever made my mother make.

I wandered through this group of kids I was going to spend the week with. I was an eleven-and-three-quarters-year-old *girl* with the body of an eight-and-three-quarters-year-old *boy* with two mosquito bites on his chest. I was at least a half foot shorter than every other kid here. Every kid but Stephanie. I finally saw her.

"Stephanie!" She felt so safe, only being one inch taller than me, and watching her get out of her car was a vision of comfort. I quickly walked through the fuzzy dandelions to get to her, not even considering my terrible allergies.

"I'm so glad you're here!" I hugged her.

"Hey! Uh, yeah." She was confused because obviously I'd never hugged her before. I wasn't even sure what had come over me, I was just so happy to see her.

"Stephanie, everyone here is old, but one cute guy already likes me!"

"What do you mean?"

"They're like grown-ups here, Stephanie!"

She laughed. "No."

Very seriously, lowering my voice so her mother can't hear from the car, I said, "They're all in junior high school *already*. We're the youngest and smallest people here. And someone already teased me about it."

Stephanie pulled her pink sleeping bag from the trunk and I tried not to be engulfed by my jealousy.

"Someone teased you!?" she asked, shocked. "What did they do?"

"It was some hairy guy who called me a toddler! The guy who defended me is cute, I swear, like a really young Ted Danson with a shaved head. I'll show him to you. Come on."

My envy left me as I began to restructure my reality into one that basically involved me and the cute guy, falling in love, away from parents, away from everything in this tiny church camp in the middle of nowhere.

As Stephanie said good-bye to her mom, I realized I was kind of upset about the very scenario I had actually come to summer camp to experience. I had come here to experience the "grown-up" teenage stuff and my first taste of it had made me uncomfortable? I needed to get over it. I was stronger than that. That guy's joke about me being little wasn't that bad. I really was okay. All I needed to focus on was the cute guy and me and our future babies.

I shut my eyes and shook my head a little, like my brain was an Etch A Sketch. Just shake it and blank. Nope. Didn't work.

"Come on, let's find out where our cabin is!"

While walking with Stephanie to the table for cabin assignments, I considered this strange feeling that had come over me. It was a sensation I'd never had before, and it wasn't just the tease. My usual enthusiasm for life was now completely absent. That would have been weird enough in any environment, but here I was, *at summer camp,* and everything was aesthetically right! The cabins, the field, the lake, the kids, it was all I'd ever hoped for. Except for this weird feeling. That was really something very strange. Something uncomfortable that I'd never felt before and I couldn't Etch A Sketch away.

"Stephanie, I feel weird."

"Like sick? I ate a bad hot dog last week and I think some of it is still stuck in me."

"Gross. Yeah, sort of like that though. I feel . . . not as excited as I was before coming here."

"It'll be fine. This place is going to be cool. Do you know where the bathrooms are?"

"Between the girls' cabins and the boys' cabins. I saw the signs on the doors while I was scoping out the boys."

Kids were beginning to move out of the field and toward their cabins to unpack and set up. I felt like they were ants dragging what they thought was food back to the nest but was really poison. Once we unrolled these sleeping bags, it would mean we were staying . . . who knew what terrible things could happen in a week? We'd only been there fifteen minutes and already it was terrible; nothing was the way I'd fantasized! Stephanie and I dragged our large duffel bags behind us as we moved through the dispersing crowd to the table where we would be assigned our cabins.

"Names?"

A very large, friendly-looking man sat at a large foldout table in a white plastic chair. He wiped dripping sweat from his forehead with the bottom of his green camp T-shirt, revealing all the rolled edges of his white stomach. I knew I should look away, but I couldn't stop staring. It was like looking at a car crash; my eyes were magnetized to his perfectly doughy, white-enough-to-burn–my-corneas stomach rolls. Stephanie was staring, too, but shouted "Stephanie Dern!" to ease the awkwardness of gazing at his giant wet nipples.

He slowly pulled his wet shirt down to end the show, curtains closed. I lifted my gaze to his look of skepticism. Oh, God, he knew I was a heathen like Anne Shirley of *Anne of Green Gables*. "Oh, hi." I smiled.

The man returned my smile and then slid the same exact style camp shirts as the one he had just mopped his sweat on across the table to Stephanie and me.

"Okay, got it," he said. "Stephanie Dern, you're cabin number three."

"I'm there, too. My name is Kelly Oxford." I smiled

again and unrolled my camp shirt. "Oh, this is a medium. I'm a small or extra-small. I need a different one. I could get lost in this shirt. I may drown in it. The collar will be so wide that it will fall and show my b-o-o-b-s." *You spelled boobs,* my own stern voice echoed in my head. *Don't let him know you know you have boobs!*

The camp man's face lost its last remaining ounce of friendliness, and everything fell into a blob of sweaty Jabba-face. It was terrifying. Even his voice dropped. "We only have one size. Stephanie, you're in cabin three, and Kelly . . ."

I guess sometimes people think I'm annoying. I get that. I talk a lot and I'm very emotional. I'm kind of an avalanche in the way that I just arrive without warning and smother you and maybe kill you.

"I have to wear an adult medium? Can I look through the pile to see if there's—"

He lifted his damp hand from the cabin list and placed it coldly on top of my hand on the T-shirt pile. "There are only mediums."

"Medium adult?"

"Yes."

"At a kids' camp?"

"Yes."

My eyes widened. "I'm going to look like I shrank! Can I wear my own shirt?"

"No."

"Can I get my hand out?" I pulled my tiny, suffocated hand out from under his.

"Kelly, you are not in cabin number three, you are in cabin number five."

I looked at Stephanie, like she would have an answer. She shrugged.

"Wait, wait," I continued to complain. Here came the avalanche. "We should be in the same cabin . . . sorry, what's your name?" I straightened my spine and tried to pull off my best "demanding mom" since my mom had left prematurely before getting this fixed.

"Geoffrey, with a *G*."

"Geoffrey with a *G*, there has been a mistake. Stephanie Dern and I should be in the same cabin. Stephanie with an *h*, and Kelly with a *y*. We should be in the same cabin. We came together."

"Um, no." Geoffrey corrected me. "I saw you. You came in a Volvo station wagon and she came in a Ford station wagon. If you want to be in the same cabin, you'll have to find a girl in one of your cabins who is willing to swap bunks, then come find me to confirm the reassignment. Got it, Kelly with a *y* and Stephanie with an *h*?"

I got the adrenaline rush and my eyes welled with emotion again as I began to step away from Geoffrey, and put on my giant shirt. It landed at my knees. I whispered to myself, "That wasn't very Christian of you, Geoffrey!"

"Next!" he called.

"Shit." I dragged my bag behind me, getting dandelion fluff and seed stuck in the cotton as Stephanie and I headed toward the row of small cabins. "Well, this sucks. He reeeeeeally sucked."

"I'm sure someone will want to switch. Everyone just got here, so no one cares yet." Stephanie nodded her head. "Besides, our cabins are pretty close, so if we aren't in the same one, it won't be a big deal."

"Stephanie, no! Why are you being so calm about this! We are supposed to be together! We're supposed to stay up all night in the cabin and talk! And put some kid's hand in warm water and make her pee, only now that I see we are the youngest kids here, that kid will probably be me, and that is *way* more likely to happen if we aren't in the same cabin! I can't be the hand-in-warm-water-pee kid. These are not the stories I want to collect for my entry into junior high school!"

As we approached the long row of cabins, I realized they were much smaller than they appeared from the car. Up close, they looked like shacks. I was worried that a shack this small could not hold the amount of insecurity I was hauling in with me.

"These cabins look like my lawnmower shed," Stephanie mumbled to me.

"Jesus never needed much," I said, in a last-ditch effort to Pollyanna the situation.

These weren't the big, fancy log cabins from my camp fantasies. These were prefab "cabins" with a window on either side of the door.

"There's cabin five." Stephanie pointed to a cabin with a group of girls standing around it, and on the right of my cabin was the washhouse, but *even more* to the right, on the *other* side of the washhouse, were the cabins with all of the boys standing around in front of them.

"Oh my God." My hands began to tingle from the adrenaline. "My cabin is right beside the boys' cabins. I'll find someone in my cabin that wants to switch so you can come to mine. Okay?"

"Got it."

"Unpack and then come see me!" I yelled as she walked toward her cabin. I heard laughter again, and it was the hairy guy. He was standing beside my lawnmower shed, with a Korean kid and Ted Danson. He was staring at me and laughing; Ted and the Korean kid were talking.

I put my bag down and swatted a mosquito from my leg, below my T-shirt hem. While taking a long look at the hairy one in the drunk smiley face T-shirt, I realized he was the Corey Feldman of the group. Always acting like an adult, a little too smart, too funny for his own good. Also very small for his age. Much like the cabins, the closer I got to him, the smaller he became. His shirt looked just as dumb on him as mine did on me. I wished Stephanie hadn't left me.

I smiled stupidly at Ted Danson dreamboat, who quickly turned and walked away.

"Shit!" I swore, feeling that familiar mosquito sting and swatting it away from my legs.

"It's a mosquito," he said mockingly.

"I'm allergic."

"Hi, Allergic, I'm Adam." Adam flicked his matted-looking longish hair to the side.

"Kelly."

The Korean kid speaks up. "I'm Tim."

He's cute, too.

"Where are you guys from?" I asked, even though my soul mate Ted Danson was no longer there and I was certain that he was really the only one who would get me. "Are you guys from around here?" I asked, and Tim raised his hand.

"Cool, I have a cabin here but I'm from Edmonton."

"Edmonton, weeeelllll," Adam whined in a lady voice. Tim laughed. "Oh la, la, Edmonton *and* a cabin! Isn't that speeecial!" Adam held his hands effeminately under his chin.

"Oh!" I laughed, stopping short of him and kicking at some dandelions. "The Church Lady. I love *Saturday Night Live*. Isn't she speeeeeecial." I laughed.

"Great for you," Adam suddenly said, cold again . . . Man, Adam was hard to read.

"So where are you from, Adam?"

"Bowden."

I laughed, hard enough that I bent slightly at the waist, and wide enough that I felt it necessary to cover my mouth (even though my teeth were straight). "Wow!"

Adam's eyes shifted to Tim and back; suddenly he looked uncomfortable. "What?"

"Well, sorry," I apologized. "I just didn't realize anyone other than convicts actually lived there. That's where the big prison is, on the highway? And, like, some flags and a water tower. Man, that's smaaaaaaall town." Subtlety was never my strong point, but I'd never met anyone from a town that small.

Adam's eyes narrowed like an animal's. "Yeah, the jail is there. It's medium-security, but there is a town, too."

"Cool." I rolled back onto my heels just enough to look taller but not enough to fall over. "Have you been here before? This camp? I haven't . . . I'm already slightly disappointed."

Adam smirked and turned away, walking toward the bigger group of guys he was with before. "'Bye, Smelly, you have huge glasses."

Wow, what a dick. I shrugged my shoulders at Tim, smiled, and turned away from them both. Suddenly I remembered how dogs rank, alphas and submissive bitches . . . I was not a submissive bitch. I mean, I've always been uncomfortable in my own skin, but I wasn't gonna get pushed around.

I called back over my shoulder, "Adam, you're a jerk from a jail town!"

He looked at me. "What?"

"You heard me. And you look just as stupid as I do in that shirt."

I grabbed my bag quickly, like it was possible for me to easily pick up, but it was too heavy and my arm jammed, so I dragged it behind me, my ant poison, heading for the door of cabin 5.

"Does someone have a cigarette? Hey, you!"

I ignored the girl's voice from the cabin as I entered because it was saying something I refused to acknowledge. I would never have a cigarette. I didn't like Mötley Crüe. I was totally focusing on finding an empty bed and not standing in the doorway any longer than I had to. I looked around the tiny dim cabin for empty bunks, and the only one that was empty was the bottom bunk to my right, beside the door.

"I SAID, HEY! HEY YOU! FOUR EYES!" It sounded more like "Foooour aies." A very thick rural Canadian accent. Strong *o*, strong *y*.

I was going to die here.

I threw my stuff onto the bed, relieved not to have to carry it anymore, sealing my fate with this hoser ant queen.

"Kaitlyn, that's rude." Another voice from another bunk. This was beginning to feel like a scene from a correctional facility.

"Oh-KAY, Oh-KAY SORRRRE-Y, YOOU!" I looked up and saw a pointy-faced girl with big curly hair, half naked and hanging off her bunk.

"Yes, you. You have any cigarettes?"

I looked around the room at the three full bunks, all girls who could be in a bad-girls' *Facts of Life* episode with a losing-your-virginity theme.

"Funny." I forced a laugh and pushed my glasses up on my face. "So um, hi, are you guys all friends? Or . . ." I was thinking about Stephanie and wondering which one of these girls would be willing to trade.

"What are you, retarded?" another girl asked. "She asked if you had smokes."

"Oh my God, Brandi, look at her." Kaitlyn rolled onto her side, letting her butt hang out in my direction. "She doesn't smoke. She's four years old."

I felt my body begin to tremble. I was angry but trying

to calm down. I invoked some Oprah-like thinking about calmness and other people's thoughts not bringing you down as I stood up, smiling, and ran out of the cabin.

I could still hear them giggling as I turned to the right and looked for cabin 3, brushing shoulders with groups of girls with boobs and perms along the way.

The door to cabin 3 was shut. (I hadn't even noticed if my cabin had a door.) I knocked and waited, crossing my arms over my nearly nonexistent boobs. The door opened; it was Stephanie, looking as upset as I felt.

"Can you get someone to switch with me?" she asked without hesitation.

"I don't think I can. They seem to already be a brothel of rural sisters, bound by sins I can't even comprehend," I said, my voice cracking. "Can you get someone to switch?"

"No. I asked and they ignored me," Stephanie whispered sadly, as the older girls yelled and laughed.

"What are we supposed to be doing anyhow? Unpacking until when? We don't even have counselors in our cabins to tell us what to do or supervise us." Stephanie stepped out the door, out of earshot of her shackmates.

She whispered, "Crystal, the girl on my top bunk, she was complaining that dinner is going to be too late tonight because of late drop-offs. She says she's a hunter, and says she's really hungry and gets mean when she's hungry. She's giant." I took Stephanie's small cold hands in mine.

I matched my whisper to hers. "Stephanie, that's really mean. Some people are naturally bigger than others. They can't help it. Look at Oprah. You can't judge her."

"No, I mean, she's like, tall like my dad. I just don't want her bunk to break and fall and crush me in the middle of the night. That's fair, right?"

I nodded yes, and looked at the Swatch on my wrist, an extravagant present from Mom last Christmas.

I suddenly had a weird pang in my stomach; it wasn't a hunger pang. "We have half an hour until dinner. Let's go to the beach."

Stephanie and I were the only two people at the camp interested in sitting on the dock on the water.

"We have it all to ourselves, at dusk, no less," I said without thinking, like I was a fifty-year-old white woman in Boca just wanting a little quiet for God's sake.

Stephanie and I both sat in silence on the end of the dock, looking across the bay. "I see my cabin." I suddenly felt sick and sad. I tried to block out the encounters with Adam, the massive nipples on Geoffrey, the dad-size shirt, and the roadhouse girls in my cabin. I tried to block them out with that one nice moment with Ted Danson, but I couldn't because Danson really ditched me on the second go-around.

"The girls in my cabin were really bad and really rude to me."

"They were?" Stephanie looked shocked.

"Are you really surprised? I'm an outcast who talks too much. Adam was kinda nice to me and I basically insulted his whole town. Look at me!"

Stephanie shrugged. "That's true. I just don't understand how everyone here is so awful."

"I don't understand how we're all just free to do whatever we want. Wait. What if this is like a reform camp, for bad kids. Bad kids who need Jesus!"

"My sister had fun here."

"Maybe Esther has a real bad streak we don't know about." I swore I'd investigate further into this theory when we returned home.

Stephanie sighed. "This place is awful."

I nodded, thinking about the lack of organization and the group of scary campers, and tears filled my eyes. "They asked me for cigarettes, called me Four Eyes, *and* managed to call me a baby in one sentence, and then their leader flashed me her big butt. Stephanie, I don't think this place is holy. I am not even religious, but I think this place is bad news."

"I'm sure they weren't trying to be mean to you. They couldn't have been," she said. I tilted my head back, hoping my tears would just pool and vanish into my eyeballs somehow. I tasted the salty snot pouring down the back of my throat and into my mouth.

Then Stephanie said it, and everything pieced together at once. "I think I'm homesick."

I gasped . . . homesickness.

"I think I am, too." I realized I'd never been apart from my family for more than a night, and even then I was at my grandparents' house. "I've never missed my mom so much in my life. I met a boy from a prison town. I was asked for cigarettes and I saw a bum."

"I just want to go home." Stephanie was now crying flat out. I didn't look at her. She deserved her space.

"I mean, don't we have counselors in our cabins?! This is going be like *Lord of the Flies,* isn't it?"

She nodded and sucked the mucus back up her nose. "I don't want to be Piggy." Her eyes pinched shut and tears fell.

"Stephanie, you could never be Piggy because you have me." I felt like that was a very supportive thing to say, like something Oprah might say to Gayle.

I looked back out across the lake to my cabin, and I could have sworn I saw my mom hugging my sister. I stopped wishing my tears would soak back into my head and let myself cry fully, too. Stephanie and I sat there like little babies, crying on the dock, until the dinner bell began to ring. We instantly began to compose ourselves, drying our faces.

"Let's stay together during dinner. I think we'll be okay. They aren't all that bad, that Ted Danson boy was nice to me, I'm sure other kids will be like us, and will like us. And I took drama classes. I can *act* cool. Everyone in my school thought I was cool!"

"I had a really good mark in drama last year." Stephanie sniffed optimistically, nodding quickly while she tucked a curl of red hair behind her ear. "I can act, too."

"Okay. We'll be okay." I helped her to her feet. "Just follow my lead," I said (as though Stephanie had a choice).

After piling macaroni and cheese onto a paper plate, I headed over to an empty table, Stephanie following close behind. The dining hall was large, white, with hanging bright lights and caged windows: nothing like the camp dining halls from the movies, and everything like jail dining halls from the movies. It was institutional, but at least not dirty.

Stephanie and I sat at the empty table and were picking at our food when the girls from my cabin walked in. Kaitlyn was now wearing clothing, or maybe I should say "clothing," because her shorts were basically inside her butt cheeks. I couldn't imagine my mom letting me even own a pair of shorts like those. It dawned on me that part of my homesickness was due to the fact that I wasn't ever allowed to watch TV shows as risqué as the "Christian" environment I was now immersed in for an entire week. The thought began to give me the sweats. I had to remember my plan of fake bravado. I needed to Pollyanna this, right now. Stephanie and I were going to be fine. I was just here to learn a lot before I entered junior high, and this whole thing could make me very street smart. Wasn't that the reason I wanted to come here? To kiss a boy and grow up a bit? This could be great. I was basically going from eleven to eighteen in a week, right? This was my dream, was it not?

Kaitlyn and Amber walked around the hall without getting any food, stopped at our table, and sat down.

"Hey," Stephanie said, very cool. (Oh, she really *was* a good drama student. She and I weren't privy to knowing everything about each other. Summer friends, you know? She was acting very cool, but I was probably better.)

"Yeah," I said, very, very coolly. "Hey."

Kaitlyn made a weird choke-laugh at me that momentarily left me wondering if her shorts were climbing higher into her butthole.

"Oh my God. Four Eyes, were you crying? Amber, look, Four Eyes was crying. Awwww. Look at her red eyes!" Amber pointed at me and then at Stephanie, chiming in, "Oh my God, look at them, they were both crying. Look at their eyes!"

I felt anger rising in me, and I made a vow. We had been driven into the camp by our mommies and we were the Piggys but now, now we would not be Piggys. I refused to be submissive. The girls' teeth flashed, they were laughing that hard. I put my fork down onto the white pile of pasta on the white plate.

"Can you two keep it down, gawwwwd?" I used my harshest but quietest, most condescending tone, the one I had perfected on my younger sister.

Kaitlyn dramatically clasped her water-balloon-like right boob. She and Amber looked at each other in mock shock.

"Does Four Eyes speak?" Kaitlyn's voice lilted up, while her head dropped down to face mine. I met her eye contact with the very best of my elementary-level drama verve.

"My name is Kelly," I hissed, "and keep your *fucking* voice down, *God damn* it." I looked around me, suspiciously, for dramatic effect. And even though I was terrified, and riding an adrenaline high like I'd never known, it was working. Kaitlyn, Amber, and Stephanie were totally hypnotized by this fog of mystery I had released with every movement, every sound I was making. Then I went in for the punch.

"We weren't crying, you permed idiot." I paused, worrying maybe I'd gone too far. But I made a quick side glance at Stephanie and saw that her false bravado was totally in synch with my own, which only made me feel more weirdly self-assured. I went for it.

"We weren't *crying*, we were *getting high*. Smoking weed."

"Yeahhhhhhh . . ." Stephanie coolly breathed. I'd never had a better improv partner, and was so grateful to her for pulling her weight at this critical moment.

My thinking was this. Seeing as though 1.) there were no counselors in our cabins and 2.) I was going to be spending time asleep with these girls in my presence, totally and completely unprotected from them, I really did have to come up with some sort of defense early on. I wasn't entirely sure that posing as a pothead would make a great long game to fight their bullying, but it certainly covered up the crybaby scenario well.

"Is that why you were acting totally retarded when you came in the cabin earlier?" Amber whispered, smiling. I nodded, because what else could I do?

"Oh my God, do you have any more?" Kaitlyn smiled, leaning in to the table toward us. I sat back the moment she leaned in. Power move.

"For you two? Yeah, right," Stephanie scoffed. I picked my fork back up, and shook my head back and forth, with superiority. I stabbed my macaroni with the fork and stuffed my mouth full, like a boss. Like I meant business. *I'm an animal, girls, step the fuck off.* But, like, I could immediately tell I'd put way too much macaroni in my mouth.

That's when Adam, Tim, and Ted Danson showed up, and like magnets, Kaitlyn's nice water-balloon boobs and Amber's attention diverted from us to them. I took that moment to pick up my napkin and spit at least half a cup of macaroni into it. Total toddler move.

"Hi, boys," Kaitlyn purred. Oh, good, I was going to get a lesson in flirting! From my power-seat, laid-back position in my chair, napkin full of bland macaroni in my lap, I studied how Kaitlyn was touching her hair, coiling it around her index finger like a phone cord. Amber absentmindedly pulled a Maybelline Kissing Kooler from her fanny pack. Cherry cola, my favorite. She put it on while staring at the boys, methodically, like a hunter looking through a scope.

Adam laid his hands on the table. His jagged nails were disgustingly lined with dirt and eaten down to the quick. His cuticles were definitely infected. I looked away.

"What are you girls doing here, all alone?"

"We aren't alone, *Adam*." I stated the obvious. "These are my roommates, Kaitlyn and Amber. Kaitlyn and Amber, this is Adam, Tim, and . . ." I looked over at Ted Danson and smiled. "What's your name?"

Ted Danson smiled back. The whiteness of his teeth was magnified by his perfect 10 tan. He was such a babe, Corey Haim had nothing on him. "It's Joe."

"And Joe." I wanted to add, "And by the way, Joe is mine," but decided that wasn't the right strategy for my camp character. My character is bold, but she hides her cards. She doesn't need to let anyone know who she wants, she just gets him. As I thought this, I accidentally winked at Joe. He looked justifiably confused.

"Are you ladies going to be around tonight?" Adam was trying to be really cool, so cool he was looking right down Kaitlyn's clinging V-neck sweater into the hole between her water balloons.

I slid sideways and put my legs up on the bench. "Where else would we be, *Bowden*?" Ooh, I'd just improv'd a nickname. "It's camp. We're here all week." Tim and Joe laughed immediately, knowing the nickname referenced Adam's little prison town, and the girls laughed, too. I suddenly felt a hot flash of dirty shame. Adam narrowed his eyes at me.

"Ha, ha, ha, not. See you later, Smelly."

"Shhh!" I said, "Don't tell everyone." I'd turned his rhyming nickname for me into another notch on my coolness totem. Total power move.

"Oh my God, Kelly." Kaitlyn was looking at my legs on the bench.

"What?" I quickly transferred the napkin full of macaroni onto my plate.

"Your legs are crazy hairy. Don't you shave?" I looked down at my legs. They *were* shaved. My mom had taught me how to shave at the beginning of the summer and I was really good at it.

Rubbing my calves, I chided her gently, "They are shaved, Kaitlyn."

"She means your thighs," Stephanie said, so flatly it was

like her roommate had actually broken the bunk bed and crushed her. I looked at my thighs. Sure, there was hair on them, but my mom had told me specifically NOT to shave my thighs or the hair would grow in thicker. I looked up at Stephanie, wondering why she'd said this, why she'd improv'd too far. I mean, why did Stephanie know what Kaitlyn was talking about? Had Stephanie been secretly judging my hairy thighs all summer?

"Yeah," Kaitlyn said, "you should shave them. You have dark hair."

"Duh." I swung my furry legs under the table, away from the judgment, away from the glaring, lamp-shaded light-bulbs hanging from the ceiling.

"I just forgot, I guess. Stoner moves." I shrugged. "No biggie, Stephanie." I made a face at her, because what the hell, she'd been thinking all this time I should shave my thighs and never told me?!

A camp counselor climbed up on a chair and whistled with her fingers in her mouth. While she explained and assigned all of the cleanup duties and lights-out policy, I rubbed the fuzz on the outside of my thighs, slightly obsessing over the criticism. I mean, I was really obsessing over the criticism. But my mom had genuinely told me to shave only to my knees! She told me it was better to leave the thighs alone! Life lessons, Kelly. Life lessons. This is why you are at camp, to learn that your mom is old-fashioned and you are supposed to shave your thighs. Calm down; your heart does not have to be beating out of your chest over this. Just shave your thighs and get over it. The counselor needed help getting down from the chair, and Tim offered. I looked at him again. He was really nice and had great hair. He used gel, but not too much.

"So," Stephanie asked, "what are we supposed to do tonight?"

Kaitlyn raised her eyebrows. "Let's get stoned."

"Oh my God. All you do is ask us for stuff," I reprimanded her. "Didn't you bring anything interesting with you, Kaitlyn? Why are you asking me for my pot and my cigarettes? What did you bring, other than your boobs and naked butt?" We all laughed at that, which was basically an auditory high-five. I had said "naked butt." I was also secretly laughing a little at the notion that I would have pot or cigarettes.

"Oh!" Kaitlyn clapped her hands like a trained seal. "I brought makeup and a body wave kit."

Wait, a body wave kit? Things were suddenly coming up Kelly.

STEPHANIE SAT ON THE edge of the sinks, resting her hairless thighs on the Formica countertop, swinging her hairless calves under the sink. Playing with my currently blown-out, stick-straight hair, I watched Kaitlyn finish up the mix of chemicals, which were wafting toward me and stinging the inside of my nose.

"Oh, God, this burns my eyes!" Kaitlyn laughed.

"That means it's eating the outer layer of your eyeball."

"Kelly, you're the nerdiest stoner I've ever met." Kaitlyn put the chemicals on the counter.

Stephanie added, "She loves *Cheers*. Kelly, do you identify with Cliff more than Norm?"

"What?" I was very confused. Between the legs and now this Cliff Clavin insult, it appeared Stephanie was conspiring against me.

"Stephanie, can I talk to you for a second?" I motioned for Stephanie to follow me outside.

"Oooooooooooo," Amber mocked as Stephanie hopped off the sinks and walked out of the washhouse.

Outside, I kept my voice low. "What is happening?"

"I don't know, you called me out here."

"Why did you make fun of my thighs and call me Cliff Clavin?"

She looked confused. "When did I make fun of your thighs?"

"You pointed out that they were hairy."

"Noooo, *they* did." Now I was confused. Was I the crazy one, or was she? Weren't we just crying together by the lake?

"You said it, too."

"What's wrong with you?"

"I just feel like you are sabotaging me a little bit."

"You're being paranoid. Besides, I don't have to agree with everything you say."

"Um, I didn't *ask* you to agree with me about everything."

"You just don't want me saying anything about you." Oh no, I was getting confused.

"Well, I mean, I don't want you to say anything mean about me! You're my friend."

"You're really sensitive." Stephanie walked back into the washhouse and I could feel an emotion wave come over me again. I tilted my head back and tasted the salt in my throat. And soon, chemicals seeping into my scalp.

"This hurts so much!"

I hit the painted cinder block wall of the girls' bathroom with my open palm. My hair was soaked in chemicals and wound up in bendy Styrofoam worms. The perm solution was definitely burning me. "It's going to look amazing on you," Amber said, exhaling smoke from a cigarette she'd bummed off a random guy in cabin 7 and blowing it right into my face. My mom's baby oil tanning was going to give her skin cancer, and my body wave week at camp was going to give me lung cancer. Stephanie and Kaitlyn had snuck off to find snacks in the kitchen after Stephanie convincingly feigned having the munchies "so, so bad."

I looked at myself in the mirror. "My mom is going to kill me."

Amber laughed. "My mom would have killed me if I did that when I was eleven, too."

"I'm almost twelve."

She exhaled her cigarette into little rings.

"How did you learn that?!" I nearly shouted. "By smoking a thousand cigarettes??" She shrugged. "Probably. I don't know."

I tried not to stare at Amber's boobs as they jiggled, but her boobs were bigger than my mom's, and to me that just seemed insane.

"How old are you?" I asked.

She exhaled the rest of the smoke and broke up the rings midair, like a collision.

"Fourteen."

Amber had long, brown, wavy hair that fell down past her big boobs. I already knew there was no way my boobs would ever be that big at fourteen. Her face was pretty—not pageant pretty, but she had nice green eyes.

"This is really hurting my head."

She looked at her Swatch.

"Close enough. Come here, I can help rinse you out."

I leaned over the sink and welcomed the relief of the cold water on my burned scalp.

Amber asked, "So, do you have a boyfriend or . . . ?" I found the question terribly disconcerting. She didn't even know where I lived, what my last name was, what I liked, what my hopes (calm, kind life) and fears (chaos) and life goals (becoming Oprah) were.

"No, but do you want to know who my hero is? It's Oprah."

Amber laughed, confused. "I didn't have a boyfriend when I was eleven either. Some of the boys here are cute, though."

"Joe is cute. That guy who is hanging out with Tim and Adam?"

"Oh, yeah. He's okay. Ugh, these chemicals are burning my eyes now."

From my upside-down view inside the sink, I could see Stephanie's and Kaitlyn's legs coming into the bathroom. I could hear them, but had no idea who was talking.

"What?"

"You weren't supposed to rinse it out for another five minutes."

"It was burning her."

"So?"

"That just means it's working, Amber."

"It will be fine. I'm going outside for fresh air. Those chemicals are harsh."

I pulled my head out from under the faucet and as I wrapped my thin peach-colored lake cabin towel around my head, I saw Stephanie and Kaitlyn, together. Stephanie was holding a cigarette. A lit cigarette. And Kaitlyn was smoking one. I tried not to look as horrified as I felt. Stephanie's mounting betrayal was as certain as her future date with emphysema.

"It's not going to work now. You totally fucked up the body wave." Kaitlyn bitched while looking at herself in the mirror. "You totally wasted that body wave kit, Kelly. You owe me thirteen dollars and ninety cents. Totally fucked the body wave."

"I think it's fine, Kaitlyn," I mumbled.

"Stephanie, how long have you guys been best friends?"

Stephanie scrunched her face up. "We aren't best friends, we only hang out during the summer. We're like lake neighbors, basically." I was horrified.

"Oh, that makes more sense." Kaitlyn took a long drag from her cigarette.

A few other girls entered the bathroom and started to talk to Kaitlyn at the mirrors.

I opened my eyes really wide at Stephanie and nodded to the right, motioning for her to go into the hall where the stalls were, and quick-stepped, peach turban bobbing, past the row of toilet stalls emanating the hard-hitting combination stench of urine, feces, and lake scum. I spun around to face Stephanie, and manically whispered, "What is happening? What are you doing with that cigarette, you have deathly asthma!"

I was on tiptoe, holding the turban up with one hand, pointing at her lit cigarette with the other.

"I'm not inhaling, it's fine. I've done this before. Calm down, let's go dry your hair in the cabin."

She's done this before?! Stephanie began to walk away.

"Stephanie, get back here!" I hissed. She rolled her eyes and walked back.

"Just an hour ago you were crying on the dock."

"So?"

"So, it made me cry. I missed my cabin, I missed everything. Even my little sister!"

"So?"

"So, what? Now you're smoking?!"

"I'm not inhaling. Look, you're the one who said we weren't going to end up as Piggy. I'm doing my part. You are being a spaz."

"Do you think there will be counselors, though? I'm honestly still a little worried."

"Of course there will be counselors. What do you think we're going to do all day? Calm down and let's have some fun." Stephanie spun on her heels and walked away.

I registered this, this moment with the cigarette and Stephanie telling *me* to calm down. Was she still improvising? If so, brava, little Elizabeth Taylor.

I'd come to this camp with her, as my one person, the one person who was in my circle of trust. What did I really know about her anyhow? Who was she when she wasn't at the lake? One more strike and I would mentally knock her out of the circle. And then I'd have no one. I had to prepare myself.

I followed Stephanie back down the hall of stinking toilets and saw that I was the only one left in the bathroom. I walked to the doorway, holding my turban up, and observed all the teens wandering around and socializing. Someone had the Eagles playing on the radio, and God, I hated the Eagles. Most of the kids were hiding cigarettes by holding them pointed up, along their arms. I wasn't sure who they were hiding the cigarettes from, there were still no grown-ups in sight. Maybe it was a habit; you know, when you're a child smoker, you probably have to have an array of devious tricks.

Stephanie stood close to Kaitlyn, laughing at something Kaitlyn was saying, pretending to smoke her cigarette, like an idiot. Adam was desperately trying to get Kaitlyn's attention, but she wasn't giving him the time of day. Tim looked over and smiled at me. I waved at him just as someone ran past the bathrooms, squealing.

I focused on the movement. It was Amber, her long, wavy hair in the wind, her sweatshirt filled with giant bouncing boobs as she ran, and there, behind her, chasing her, was

Joe. I watched, breathlessly, as he swept her up from behind. Both of them were laughing like I'd never seen teenagers laugh. She turned, into his arms, looked up, and I watched them kiss. I watched her get my kiss. Right there, in front of me, she was kissing the guy I had told her I liked, the guy she wasn't interested in. I let go of my turban and it fell to the ground, with half of my hair still in it.

"IT'S GOING TO BE fine," Amber said as she assessed my perm, pulling chunks of my hair right off. I turned to the door, toward the sound of snickering, and saw Adam.

"GET OUT." Stephanie slammed the door on him.

There was lots of hair on the floor. I hadn't looked in the mirror yet. I never wanted to look in a mirror again. I was crying hard in Cabin 5. I'd disobeyed my parents, bodywaved my hair, and now I was going bald at the hands of the Jezebel who stole the only boy I cared about. My soul mate. One moment she was kissing my Ted Danson, and the next, she was pulling my hair from my head. This was the worst day of my life. I never should have shown my cards to Amber, or told her about Joe; rookie move, Oxford, rookie move.

"We should cut it." Kaitlyn took the base of my head into her hands and tilted my whole head like it was a bowling ball.

"It's only breaking at your shoulders, you're fine." She dropped my head. "My cousin had this happen and it came off at the scalp. People thought she was going full Sinéad O'Connor. Full-blown dyke."

"Sinéad O'Connor isn't gay," I stated, but I was really thinking, *Oh, dear God, I don't want to go full Sinéad O'Connor.*

"Well . . ." Kaitlyn spat on her cigarette to put it out and the thick saliva slid off the burning orange tip onto the floor. "I mean, this happens, like, one out of every four home body waves."

"You knew this could happen, you knew my hair could fall out, and you still let me do this?" I shrieked, and slapped at a mosquito on my leg. "And who left our cabin door open anyhow? There are so many mosquitoes in here, we're never going to be able to fall asleep!"

"Kelly hates mosquitoes," Stephanie said flatly, then, sarcastically, "She's *allergic.*"

I shot a look at Stephanie, but it didn't land because she was shooting a look at the infiltrator, Kaitlyn. Stephanie was basically already outside my circle and we'd only been there three hours. At least I wasn't crying anymore.

One of my roommates, Jen, a meek Eeyore-like blonde with big curly bangs and a long, swaying ponytail, walked into the cabin with a large pair of scissors. She had already proclaimed her love for Tim. With her long, weird neck and dopey basset hound eyes, she seemed like the type of person who would either be insanely kind due to low IQ or a murdering psychopath, the offspring of first cousins.

"Camp Lady Dawn lended these to me," her spiritless voice groaned. "I lied and she gave them 'cause I told her one of you guyeses' sleeping bags' zippers was stuck."

I looked at Jen. "You aren't cutting my hair, and it's *loaned*. Not lended. And *you guyses* isn't a word."

I didn't know when to shut up.

"Jen, just give me the scissors." Amber held her hand out to Jen, who almost stupidly dropped them into her palm, sharp point down. (And Amber had called *me* retarded, twice.)

"My aunt Linda has a salon in the back of her house. I've watched her cut hair thousands of times." Amber gloated.

I composed myself, and remembered Oprah talking about all of her hair breaking off once when she went in to get it done. At least I was still following in her footsteps, even the mistakes. I mean, if I could make an Oprah-size mistake, and she turned out okay, maybe this wasn't so bad.

I didn't put up a fight as man-stealing Amber pulled a brush through my hair, broke more pieces off, and threw them aside like it hadn't taken years to grow my hair that long. Then, while I just sat there, staring, like it was an out-of-body experience, she took the scissors in one hand and cut my hair just above my shoulder line.

"There, none of it is breaking above your shoulders, right?" She was looking around the rest of my now frizzing, body-waved head. I held up some of the front pieces for her to look at. I had my dad's thin hair, the front was even thinner, and it was breaking off at nose level.

"Bangs are cute. Don't worry."

And with that, Amber grabbed the front section of my hair. She stuck her tongue out when she was concentrating, like my sister and my mom. She sectioned the hair off a second time and cut me some bangs. I could feel they were some very, very, very short bangs.

Amber stood back, with Jen, Kaitlyn, and Stephanie.

I didn't move anything but my eyeballs, and I pointed them right at Stephanie.

The look on her face was one of someone watching Linda Blair penetrate herself bloody with a crucifix.

I sat in front of them, frozen in their judgment, with no idea what I looked like.

"Yep, yep," Stephanie said. "Maybe we just need some gel and hair spray?" She looked at the other three for approval. They all agreed.

"Do you want to see?" Amber asked me.

"No, not really. I trust you guys. I think I'm going to just go to bed."

I threw myself onto my back in my bunk and pretended it was all a bad dream.

"Here. Kelly. Look at yourself. You need to see." Amber solemnly brought me a mirror from her pink backpack. I looked at the faces of my roommates. They looked worried. I exhaled. "God, really? Is it really . . ."

Then I saw myself. Only it didn't look like me.

An hour ago my hair had been all one length to my chest. Now my hair was a ball of frizz framing a pair of glasses that rested on a small nose. I had bangs cut on a slight angle, like a garage driveway, and they landed in the middle of my forehead, far from my eyebrows. I looked like a monster! I was an exaggerated Roseanne Roseannadanna. I wondered if there was a way to rewind the last hour, maybe the last twenty-four hours. I looked at my burned hair and tried not to cry as I passed the mirror back to Amber.

"Wait! I have the best hair spray, it will totally help your hair. It's like magic." Kaitlyn climbed up the bunk in her little shorts and dug around in her bag.

"Here, check this out. Magic." Kaitlyn was standing in the middle of the room holding the canister of hair spray out at full arm's length. She took a quick look.

"Is there space around me?" she asked.

Jen nodded. "Yeah."

Kaitlyn said each word so slowly, so we wouldn't miss one piece of direction: "No . . . one . . . move."

Then, with an equally drawn-out movement, she lifted a lighter and flicked it on.

No.

Kaitlyn pressed on the can of hair spray and a fireball exploded, flashing from her wiry hands. The flame was so big that I couldn't see the girls on the other side of it. In a way, I was comforted by my moment of solitude in cabin 5. For a moment, none of them existed behind that irresponsible chemical inferno. And then, as fast as it had appeared, the fireball disappeared, and they were back.

I saw the girls piled on top of each other on the floor, some with eyes wide and others with eyes squeezed closed in laughter. I rolled over, pulled my knees up, and plunged my feet into my ugly green, not pink, sleeping bag, dipping them into the depths of the cotton, and pulled the top of the bag down over my head.

"Don't do that again, you fucking moron!" Amber laughed.

"I won't, I won't," Kaitlyn giggled, with slight protest. "Hey, Kelly, did you see that?"

"Yup!" I stuck my arm out of my sleeping bag and gave her a thumbs-up.

Away from the sounds, from the mosquitoes, hiding my hair from the world inside my dark, most unfavorite sleeping bag, I thought about how simple things were when I was in my cabin, reading my books, watching my mom get cancer, making orange juice with warm water for my irritating little sister, and dreaming about summer camp instead of actually being here.

I FELT ALL EYES on me in the dining hall the next morning while I ate Frosted Flakes from my mini cereal box at the long table with Stephanie, Kaitlyn, and Amber. It really didn't help that their eyes were the closest to me, and that all six of those eyeballs were staring at my head.

"You guys can stop looking at my hair anytime now," I exclaimed, maudlin, as I dipped my spoon into the milky, sweet contents of the wax-lined box.

"It's just . . . big." Stephanie continued to stare.

"I know. I know. I look like . . ."

I felt someone touching my hair.

"Prince Valiant?" Adam had appeared out of nowhere, laughing and definitely in my personal space. He snorted, then patted me on the shoulder. "Prince Valiant, you look ridiculous."

My fake friends at the table began to laugh at my expense, but none of their laughter really cut me, except for Stephanie's. Here I was, with my stupid Roseanne Roseannadanna hair, with a bunch of kids I didn't even know who had already ruined my life. I hadn't been at camp for twenty-four hours and was already suffering the ultimate betrayal at the hands of my only summer friend. Stephanie had totally given up; she was crying on the dock way harder than I was. I was the one who gave her courage! I was the one who saved her with the plan, and now *she* was mocking *me*, in front of everyone else? If I were a lesser person I would just tell them there was no weed, she was crying. Instead, I take the high road.

"Stephanie. Fuck off." I was shaking.

The table quieted down. "Ooooooooooohhhh." Kaitlyn pushed her cereal to the side.

Adam continued to laugh.

"Is there a problem over here?" Geoffrey approached the table with the ease of a drunken ox. He was already wiping sweat from his brow at nine in the morning.

Nobody at the table answered.

"All right, you guys clear up and head to the field for arts and crafts." Before he walked away, I noticed Geoffrey do a double take of my hair.

Fuck you, too, Geoffrey with a G.

I was cursing, considering swimming home and dropping my uneaten sugar flakes into the garbage can, when Tim appeared. "It isn't that bad." He smiled.

"What isn't? MY HAIR?" I shrieked, my head suddenly feeling light.

"No, the arts and crafts project." He was still smiling. "I'm kidding"—he leaned into me—"I meant your hair. It isn't as bad as you think."

"Oh . . ." I giggled, feeling slightly in love, which I recognized immediately as a default setting on my brain to any sudden positive attention. Very troubling.

"I figured you were talking about something else, because this?"—I pointed to my hair—"is really bad." He took my tray from my hand and set it down for me.

"Thanks."

We began to walk out of the dining hall together, like a couple. I caught a glimpse of my hair in a window reflection and didn't auto-vom, and it was then that I realized Tim had cured my bad mood.

"You know, Adam is just like that. He doesn't mean anything by it."

"Right, like, how people say, 'they only tease you because they like you.' That's baloney. Can I be honest with you here, Tim?"

"Sure." He shrugged.

"People are mean."

"Yeah, they can be."

I was taking in the moment, Tim and I, walking through the dandelions. I didn't have a care in the world until I saw Jen running past us, her gait jagged and lumbering. I prayed she wouldn't fall.

"Hey, Kelly." She waved, so awkwardly I shook my head.

"Hey, Jen." She galloped by, seemingly trying not to fall with every step, though she was perfectly able.

"She your friend?" Tim asked.

I shook my head. "No, I don't really know her. She's in

my bunkhouse. She did tell me she had a crush on you, though, which is . . . sweet." I laughed at her expense as we reached the group of kids at the "meeting spot."

I spotted Stephanie; she was staring at me. I decided to join her and see if she tried to patch things up with me. This walk with Tim had really lifted my spirits. I was sure Steph wanted to apologize for being a heinous bitch.

"See you!" I turned to Tim and embraced him, like we were married. I imagined our biracial children would be very beautiful. I already had one eye that was almost Asian. A few years ago one of my sister's friends had given me the nickname "Chinese eye." It was a huge compliment. I kept hugging Tim, despite his being very stiff in my arms. In fact I piled on the love even harder and rubbed his back.

"See you later?"

"Sure . . . ?" he said, and I heard, but ignored, the hint of a question lingering in his voice.

I dropped myself into the ground beside Stephanie. "I'm not sorry I swore at you."

Stephanie said nothing.

"Everyone! Everyone SETTLE DOWN!" Geoffrey shouted with his hands on his hips.

"We're going to be making masks today with plaster wrap. Please pick a partner to work with, put lotion on your eyebrows, and grab a bucket of water and the plaster wrap from up here."

"Do you want me to get the stuff?" I asked Stephanie.

"I'm not going to be your partner." She stated this like

it was the most obvious thing in the world. "I'm partnering with Kaitlyn." Stephanie stood, I followed her. Or I was trying to follow her, but she was walking away from me so fast, I was already out of breath, and in this field of dandelion I knew it couldn't be good for my lungs.

"What? Stephanie. Are you serious?"

She didn't turn around so I stopped and scanned the crowd to see who my partner options were before I looked any more insane and let my emotions and neediness get the best of me. I saw Stephanie and Kaitlyn, already grabbing a bucket. I hated them. Then I saw Amber, the Jezebel who was with my first boyfriend, Joe. Where was Tim?

Then I saw him.

The true depths of my stupidity hit me in the face.

Tim was with Jen?!

Jen the oaf? He was with Jen, and standing so close to her that her shy, houndlike face was purple and sweating.

"Oh my God." This was truly hilarious, you know? Because first I had told Stephanie I'd help her make friends and I had, and she ended up turning on me. Then I'd told Amber who I thought was the hottest guy at camp, and she went after him. Then I'd told Tim that Jen had a crush on him, because I was being mean and spiteful and thought he would think it was silly of her.

I was a real dumb-ass. What was all of this about, Oprah? I touched my hair.

"What?" Adam was wearing a weird purple bandanna in his hair. He was also looking at Tim and Jen.

"Nothing."

"You need a partner, right? I'll take the fall and be your partner. I don't want you to look completely pathetic."

I rolled my eyes at him. "Oh my God, I'd rather drop dead than be your partner, Adam. This is the worst day of my life. I swear. I would totally drop dead right now if my mother wouldn't be left wondering if it was her fault for not letting me body-wave my hair at home, which it totally would be because I let some shorts-up-her-butt smoker girl mess it up so badly I killed myself."

"Uh . . ." Adam was confused. "You want me to get the bucket?"

ADAM LAID A SECOND layer of cold, wet plaster gauze on my face. Cotton pads were on top of my eyes, under the plaster. In the dark, things weren't so bad anymore. I pretended I was Stevie Wonder. I lay in the grass, in the dark, my nose getting stuffed from being so close to the dandelions.

"I'm not very good at this," he said.

"I'm sure it's fine."

"Good job, Adam." I heard Geoffrey's voice.

"Geoffrey, what's the point of making these masks?" Adam asked. I felt his fingertips delicately tapping the wet gauze down onto my eyeballs. I hadn't realized Adam had that delicate-touch sort of thing in him.

"Well," Geoffrey sighed, and I imagined him wiping sweat from the rolls of his neck, "after they're dry, tomorrow probably, we are going to paint and decorate the masks. You're supposed to paint the outside of the mask the way you show the world who you are, your outward mask . . .

and the inside of the mask the way you feel about yourself. Your inside mask. Or something."

"What does that even mean, man?" Adam asked, dropping another piece of wet gauze across my forehead.

"Well, we all wear masks. What's yours?"

"I don't wear a mask." Adam laughed. "I am who I am. Just like Axl Rose."

"Well, then . . ." I knew Geoffrey had walked off because I could hear his voice getting farther away. I was just like Stevie Wonder now.

"I can assure you that even Axl Rose wears a mask. You paint whatever you'd like on your mask tomorrow, Adam. I look forward to seeing what you have inside of you, too."

"Gross," Adam whispered. I giggled.

We were together in silence for a moment, then I whispered, "Geoffrey's mask would be so sweaty."

Adam chuckled. "So sweaty! I know!"

"On the inside of the mask? Sweat. On the outside of the mask? Sweat." I tried to keep my voice low, but that came out too loud.

"I shouldn't say that. I shouldn't talk about people's bodies. I can't help it, though. I'm not very nice. I think the inside of my mask will be black and gross." I joked about this, but I knew it was true. I didn't like a lot of the things I thought and did, and that was very confusing. "Also? Axl Rose is a mask, there is no way his name is Axl Rose."

"That's true," Adam said. "This is kinda fun."

"Okay, so, what is everyone else doing? I can't see a fucking thing." I was enjoying this new freedom, away from adults, away from other people looking at my hair, the freedom to say my father's favorite word.

"Masks. Tim is making one on Jen. Joe is making one on Amber."

"Stop, that sounds perverted. You almost done?"

"Making one on you?"

"I'm gonna hurl."

"Wait." I felt Adam's hand, or I assumed it was Adam's, on my shoulder. "Kaitlyn is coming over."

"Oh, you mean, the girl you have a crush on?" I was so over all of this. My emotions were going completely haywire. I felt insane. Adam and I were sort of having a moment. I was happy one second and wanted to die the next. I was going to leave this mask on forever. Paint the outside of it with "Fuck off," grow my hair down to my feet, and never hang around humans again.

"What? I don't like Kaitlyn; she's awful. I like her boobs, but that's just because I'm a guy. I hate her. She's the worst."

"Oh," I said, but I had no idea if Adam heard me. I did hear Kaitlyn laughing.

"Adam! You'll never guess what that moron Stephanie did. She gave me spices she stole from the kitchen and tried to sell it to me as pot."

Oh no.

"She did?"

"Yes."

I sat up, in my mask. "Kaitlyn, why don't you lay off Stephanie? Aren't you her friend?"

"Aw, Kelly, your hair looks so cute in that mask."

"Kaitlyn, you're a jerk for making fun of Stephanie." I tried to pull my mask off, but it was stuck. I sneezed.

"Kelly, stop. It's fine." I heard Stephanie's voice.

"Oh, look," Kaitlyn purred, "it's the drug dealer."

I faced the ground and pulled at my mask. "OW!!!!" I screamed, "WHY IS THIS STUCK?!" It suddenly popped off.

I was not sure if it was the sun or what, but above the eye pads inside the mask, I thought I could see something dark.

"Oh crap," Adam said. "The lotion."

"My eyebrows."

Most of my eyebrows were stuck in the mask instead of on my face.

My inside mask was just a pair of eyebrows.

"I'm so sorry." Adam looked at me; I could barely look up at him.

"This couldn't get any better. I mean, could it?" Kaitlyn's laugh had become the sound of hell. How many times was she going to laugh at my body hair?

"It could," I said.

"How?"

"Kaitlyn, you're a terribly mean girl. I came to camp to learn about kids in junior high school and I tried to be your friend by being a drug addict and that was just really, really stupid."

"Aww, what a little baby. Are you going to paint eyebrows on your face and flowers and lollipops on the outside of your mask tomorrow?"

"Geoffrey?!!" I shouted, and like an eager dog, he turned, head cocked to the side.

"Kaitlyn is trying to buy drugs off people, she keeps asking for drugs, she has cigarettes and tried to light our cabin on fire last night."

Every kid in the camp stopped working on masks and stared at Kaitlyn. I smiled at her, with my haircut and patchy eyebrows.

I turned to Stephanie. "See, I told you I wouldn't let you be Piggy."

I walked away from the scene behind me, but Adam caught up.

"That was cool."

"Are you trying to be my friend now that I'm a true toddler tattletale?"

"I don't know."

We walked together toward the row of cabins. I was holding my mask.

"I feel really bad about your eyebrows."

"It's fine, really. It's not like they're all gone, I have huge eyebrows," I said. "My family will think this is hilarious. I came to camp to get some street smarts and instead I lost my only friend and all my hair and will probably be murdered by a girl named Kaitlyn."

"Aw, she won't murder you. I'll protect you! Look at these muscles!" He flexed and nothing really changed in his arms. I laughed and felt a tingle for Adam, which was sort of grossing me out, because it was gross-me-out

Adam . . . but at least that was a deterrent from telling any of my friends about him so they could steal him. Yep, certifiably boy crazy.

"Your muscles are as big as my eyebrows."

"I'm so sorry. You really went batshit pulling that thing off your face."

"I was so mad. I had to get it off. I guess when I draw the inside of my mask, like, my insecurity and neediness, it will look very realistic."

Adam stepped closer to me and touched the sore spots on my face where the eyebrow hairs used to be. This was as intimate as I'd ever been with a boy while owning a set of small boobs.

"Are they gonna grow back, you think?" he asked.

"Have you seen the hair on my thighs?"

He blushed.

Silver Linings

"Do you want to make the Rice Krispie squares or not?" Miss Georgia rhythmically shook the box of cereal in my face as she glanced out the window at the dark, greenish skies of a summer thunderstorm.

Miss Georgia was the task-oriented summer day camp counselor who really liked to focus on cooking and eating but never ate a thing herself.

"No, thank you, Miss Georgia." I eyed her suspiciously

as she turned to the group of eager, drooling, prediabetic little goblins in the kitchen. These other day camp kids saw the Pied Piper, but I saw the witch in "Hansel and Gretel"; she just seemed too keen on feeding us. What were her true motives? Why keep feeding us treats after meals? It freaked me out. I hated day camp.

Besides all that Lauren was one of the sugar goblins making the Rice Krispie squares, and at this point of our summer break, I was taking any opportunity to be apart from her.

Lauren wasn't a terrible little sister or anything. The fact was, we'd been together twenty-four hours a day since school ended.

We slept in the same room, ate every meal together, rode in the car together. Frankly, I was nine and I just needed some space. We were basically cellmates in the same middle-class, working-parent prison that was this day camp.

Yes, I said it, prison. Generally, kids have no control over what food they are served, where they go, who they get to spend time with and for how long. It's all luck, you know, whether or not you'll be born to wonderful parents who are going to be acceptable "jailkeepers," terrible jailkeepers, or the very, very rarest of the rare, wealthy parents who write a letter, tear it up, throw it in the fireplace, and Mary Poppins appears. Our parents couldn't afford Mary Poppins. (To be honest, I couldn't have handled her reluctance to show affection; that was weird, right?) But they were pretty great, except . . . they did make us go to summer day care, under the guise of day camp.

I looked around the home ec room to see what other options I had that afternoon. *Day camp* was a term I was quick to call bullshit on whenever it was used. "Summer day camp" is something we lower- or lower-middle or middle-class (or maybe upper-class "let's teach you a lesson") children of working parents are well versed in. Yes, the season was summer, no, that didn't mean it was actually camp. This was glorified day care. And sure, I preferred it to abuse and abandonment, but come on . . . don't call it camp!

In May, we had been told we were going to spend most of our summer at Strathern School day camp. This was horrible news; until this point in our lives my mother had always had summers off and we were free to go to the cabin we shared with our cousins and Gram at the lake. Staying in the city was the worst news for two kids from a city that was usually covered in snow, who knew the realities of using hose water to make personal skating rinks in their backyards for nine months of the year. But the fact was, my parents had been arguing and stressed about money for months and Mom had to work. She'd already registered us. Now she had to sell us on it.

"There are movie days! Oh, a mini-Olympics, wait, cooking and singing, too?! What a great camp."

Her patter of fragmented sentence and hypervibrato shouts would not distract me. You can't spend hours watching *Murder, She Wrote* with your kid and then try to pull a fast one on them. It doesn't work.

I knew the essence of what was happening.

"Mom, it's day care." I said this in a tone the complete

opposite of hers. I was dead serious, I knew this was complete trickery, and she needed to know that I knew.

"This isn't like camp at the lake! I don't get a cute cabin, fresh lake air, meals, and sleepovers with friends. This is concrete jungle day care."

My mom was basically a stay-at-home mom, but for a few years there were stretches at the Korean day care, a place of many harsh lessons. 1.) Koreans don't fuck around. 2.) Dowager's humps are real, and if you slouch over you get them. 3.) Kimchi. After the Koreans told me I was too talkative and made me sit for twenty whole minutes in silence (!!), Mom had promised us no more day care. Now she was breaking her promise with a flimsy semantical argument.

"Sure, this place may not be being run as a North Korean Intelligence unit, but you're sending us to day care, Mom. It isn't a camp."

I'd hoped at this point my sister would speak up, fall in line, and side with me. I'd always prayed for a hype man. I mean, I slept beside her every single night, we were going to be trapped together for several more years; there should have been some camaraderie, but no. I looked over at her in her seat and she was asleep, mouth open. I sighed, knowing that even if she were awake, she was only eight and would fail to see my point anyhow.

Mom would pretend she didn't hear things when she wasn't interested in discussing them. This was her way. Or she'd completely forget things, jokingly call herself Forgetful Joe, and simply move on to another topic. Like selective Alzheimer's. I knew I was being annoying, and she was just trying to find a solution. . . . I just wanted her to empathize with me, maybe be a partner in this terrible, no-one-is-getting-to-do-what-they-want-to-do bummer of a summer.

And there I was, now a month into it, trying to find something in this child-care prison facility to occupy myself with.

While the three Michelin-star mini-chefs were in the kitchen, microwaving bowls of marshmallows, I looked around the room thinking about my options. I couldn't go outside; the sky was so dark that at 3:45 in the afternoon it may as well have been 11 p.m. and it was now hailing along with the rain, which was a very common thing in the summer afternoons of my youth.

Living in the prairies, we knew this cycle. Hot mornings, cloud-building afternoons, late-afternoon thunderstorms. Balls of ice would often fall from the sky during a storm. You could tell from the fluffiness of some clouds if they were full of hail or not, but during storms like today's—dark and angry—hail was just a given. Growing up in the prairies gave me a fondness for weather and natural disasters, because most of what I could see was the sky, and we really couldn't have earthquakes or tsunamis, lava flows or quicksand. (I realize quicksand isn't a natural disaster, but for children who grew up in the '80s, it was a huge fear.)

I saw a boy I went to school with named Nadir pulling the record player headphones off his head and ran to grab them before they hit the table. Music was one true escape for me. George Michael, you and that other slightly creepy guy from Wham!, please take me away.

"Hey, Four Eyes, slow down." In any given year of my childhood, there was always a boy picking apart my appearance, and right now, Terry, the red-haired bully, was on my case. I weighed sixty pounds, and had large glasses that magnified my eyes, so I was an easy target for low-brow humor. Adults loved to tell me loads of BS like, "He teases you because he likes you!" and "Your glasses make you cuter and that's why people tease you!" This only led me to believe that abuse and affection are intertwined. Which, you know, isn't really the best lesson to be teaching a child.

I pretended not to hear Terry, because I didn't have four eyes, I had two, and those two eyes were pretty much broken so I was honestly more like a no eyes. I dropped the needle on the saxophone solo in "Careless Whispers."

That's when Nadir's mom ran into the room, like a maniac.

There are many non-illegal things (aside from the obvious, not wanting to stumble upon your parents having sex) that children don't want to see.

Examples:

1. The sweaty inside of a lunch box.
2. A kid who eats bits of his own body. *See* boogers, scabs, fingernails, dried scalp, hair, pus, dead skin, or earwax.
3. A dog's penis.

4. Only a few presents with your name under the Christmas tree (sorry, Jewish friends, I'm not sure what the equivalent is for you but this one is pretty severe for us fake or full-fledged Christian children.)

5. Caviar, tent caterpillars, or squished tent caterpillars.

But none can raise alert, fear, or confusion faster than seeing your mother running. No one wants to see a mother run.

Many people stopped what they were doing and turned their attention to Nadir's mother when she ran in the room, because what could possibly be more important than a mother running? It was very jarring for us all; this thin woman with skin the color of almonds, wearing a large funnel-necked sweater, was more effective at getting our attention than a school's fire bell. I kept the saxophone solo playing through my headphones for a few more seconds, to relish the soundtrack layered with the panicked mother, before curiosity got the best of me and I pulled the headphones from my ears and off my head.

Nadir's mom was yelling, "It's a tornado! There is a tornado and it's going through Millwoods. Wait. Am I the first one to tell you?"

Okay. This is where I freeze up, because up until this point in my life, we'd had many tornado warnings but never an actual tornado. Maybe funnel clouds had formed, and the newspaper would run photos of them, but never a full tornado.

And, while we didn't live near Millwoods, and I wasn't

really worried about our house, I really, really didn't like the way she said, "Am I the first one to tell you?" Because, to me, that implied this situation was very bad. This situation was very bad and I was at *day care* with my little sister. I wasn't even with my parents.

Lauren quickly small-stepped her way over to me across the room from the kitchen in her fuzzy pink socks. She sat down beside me on the shag square of carpeting with a handful of marshmallows.

"Is Mom coming?" she asked.

"I guess," I said. "She doesn't pick us up until five thirty."

"But, if we're going to die from this tornado, she'll come, right?" She stuffed her mouth with a marshmallow and I wondered if Mom really was driving to come and get us. She had to be.

We had no family plan for natural disasters.

We had a plan for abduction. If a stranger were to arrive and pick us up, he needed to know the secret password, which I'd chosen myself—Tubal Ligation. But now I worried. What happened in a natural disaster when I wasn't with my mother?

My mom was working as the head nurse on a First Nations reserve just north of the city. She got to do cool things like hang out in teepees and, once, eat bannock and barbecued beaver on a stick. The job couldn't afford her a Mary Poppins, but to me she was very worldly.

"Who's coming with me?!" Terry yelled.

Nadir and his mom appeared to be gone already as Terry led a group of charging kids out the side door and into the dark, green-hued field. I'd seen green skies during storms before, but none this green.

If my mom had been there, during the tornado, she would not have allowed me to run outside. She would have had us in the basement with treats, blankets, flashlights, and CBC news blasting on the TV, and the radio because the TV goes out in bad storms and that was always my indication that a storm had escalated. TV goes out, take cover.

I grabbed Lauren's hand, stood up, and ran to the door, following Terry.

Unwillingly, Lauren ran alongside me through the doorway, bannered "Class of 1987," and suddenly we were outside in the field, the sounds of rain and wind in our ears as we stood beside the school parking lot.

"What are we doing?" Lauren yelled. "It's pouring rain! We're wearing our indoor shoes!" and finally, "There's a tornado somewhere out here!"

The rain and hail were loud and the air was suddenly very, very cold, much colder than it had been that morning when my mom laid out my shorts, which were now soaked in freezing rainwater. *This is what happens*, I thought, *this is what happens when you leave your children with strangers!*

"Kelly! It's so cold!! What's wrong with you?" Lauren squealed. "It's scary out here!"

"Fine, go back in. I'm staying outside." Again, I really wished she were more of a hype man or sidekick. I'd keep trying, for years to come, until the day of my parents' divorce, when it really mattered, and we both miraculously and naturally agreed on every single thing.

I let go of Lauren's hand and she ran back into the school, which was a lot smarter than standing in the freezing rain, but I stayed outside anyway to make a point. To prove that day camp wasn't fun or safe. Or camp.

I was completely soaked, watching the boys run through the thick, long grass and small hail pellets, laughing and screaming and tackling each other.

I was now, for this moment, alone in this world, and I knew it. Maybe my first self-aware moment, of pure loneliness. I looked up to the sky for funnel clouds, scanning the horizon for the tornado. I saw nothing but dark, fast-moving clouds with fingerlike ends reaching out and then vanishing. There I was, with no mom, no dad, no siblings, no friend to watch over me, just me in a green field under a green sky, contemplating a storm that I was positive had already killed people (it had). My mom was going to freak out when she learned that day camp was this dangerous. Her child was outside in the middle of a tornado. This was what she got for being so haphazard with her children.

SMASH!

I jumped at the sound of the broken glass and looked around, but I couldn't figure out what was broken.

THUMP.

THUMP.

I felt the ground thump beneath my indoor shoes that could no longer be indoor shoes because they were soaked through and covered with the mud I was standing in. Well, that's what my mom got, for leaving me with strangers in the middle of a tornado.

There were a couple of small bounces of movement under my feet before I located the object with my eyes, a baseball. *Where did the boys get baseballs and why are they throwing them at me?* These were my first thoughts, but also, of course, *They are throwing baseballs at me* was the next.

As I reached down for one, I noticed it was bumpy and not smooth, and it was whiter than any baseball I'd ever seen. Then I touched it. Ice.

"GET INSIDE THE SCHOOL! THIS INSTANT!" The day-camp ladies had forced the windows open and were yelling at us.

I recall this all in slow motion now, you know, the yelling and realizing that this baseball was hail and it had come down from the sky at an incredible speed. That seemed a very dangerous thing to happen while away from my loving parents at day care.

"GET INSIDE RIGHT THIS SECOND!" Miss Georgia howled. Now, if she were my parent, she would have run out into this field, picked me up, and carried me back in. Miss Georgia was doing none of that. She was basically leaving me in this field, to die.

I couldn't move. I stood, Keds sinking in the mud, watching the baseball-size ice balls slam into the grass through the green glow around me, like frozen meteors.

The boys' yelling broke my trance. I looked up and saw

Terry and his friends running to the door, his entire face was an entirely more than usual drained, pallid white from fear. He wasn't even looking at me when he shouted,

"*Four Eyes, you gonna die!*"

I think he was trying to help me in his own way, warn me of the inevitable. I couldn't be sure, because he was truly a different breed from me: a child who smoked, a Freddy Krueger fan, whereas my mom wouldn't even let me look at the VHS cover for *Sex, Lies, and Videotape* at the movie rental store across from Value Village.

"KELLY, GET INSIDE RIGHT NOW," another day-camp worker yelled.

Wow, they knew my name? Another THUMP, a baseball-size hailstone had fallen three feet away from me.

And with that last thump, I realized I could actually really die . . . right now . . . at a day camp . . . in Edmonton.

And then I broke out of the slow motion and I was running. I ran as fast as my body would move me, like I was being paid to run. This was what I like to call my Tom Cruise run.

I made my hands totally flat and kept my fingers together like my hands were pizza slicers about to cut a swath ahead of me. I pretended there was actual pizza waiting for me on the other side of the door. I stared straight ahead at the heavy wood and metal doors of the school as I ran toward them, seeing the ice balls crashing to the ground around me. I must have looked like a character in some demented, and certainly Canadian, video game. I lifted my shoulders to my ears, ready for one to hit my head and split it in half. I could see my chubby little sister, still wet from the rain, in the school window watching me run. She would see my head explode like a watermelon; it would be insane. These were the types of day-care stories that had the potential to become legend.

I made it back to the school in one shivering piece and crashed through the heavy doors, cracks of thunder booming behind me.

All the day-camp lady said was, "Kelly, don't ever do that again. You have to get new shoes for tomorrow."

Not "Nice running, great hands." Or "So glad your head didn't explode like a watermelon." Or "Want a towel, you dumb kid?"

Just a reminder that she didn't care about me at all and my mom was going to be really pissed off that she was going to have to take me to Bonnie Doon Shopping Centre and buy me a new pair of Keds.

I dried myself off with the paint smocks, a pile of old dad shirts from the 1970s, while I watched other mothers run into the building to collect their children, yelling things like:

"Well, this has been the worst day of my life."

"Why do tornadoes always have to hit trailer parks? Those people have it bad enough."

"There wasn't an explosion, but the refinery was a direct hit. Makes you wonder if they even do anything in there all day."

My mom showed up early, too, much to our relief. There were only a few of us left. I hid my shoes behind me as

Lauren and I watched the old gold Volvo station wagon pull into the parking lot.

"What are you going to do?" Lauren said, looking at my muddy, stiffening canvas shoes. I tried to redirect her train of thinking. Classic older-sibling move.

"Why are you worried about my shoes? Forget about them. We're in the middle of a natural disaster!"

My mom entered the room wild-eyed, beads of water falling from her wiry black hair. I had my father's thin British hair, and was always in awe of hers; I'd stare at it, like there was no way I could be her child.

"I had to drive in on the highway, the car was between two funnel clouds almost the entire way." That was what my mom added to the stream of mom talk when she entered the room.

"Well, I almost got decapitated from a hailstone because my mom left me at day care without a plan during a natural disaster." (I thought this but didn't dare say it.)

In the car, Mom could not stop talking about the funnel clouds.

"I thought that was it!"

Wait, she thought that was it? This terrified both my sister and myself. Moms were supposed to live forever. I mean, at least until my sister and I had kids and we made the Thanksgiving dinners . . . but she still had to be alive to clean up after we were done eating. Why did she have to add *Moms are afraid of accidentally dying* to my already growing stockpile of anxieties?

Hearing that my mom thought, even for a moment, that

she could have died was terrible. *Annie* was my favorite movie. I couldn't deal with my own imagination when it came to losing a parent. Who could replace them? No one in my town was as rich as Daddy Warbucks for me to fantasize about, no one but Wayne Gretzky. If my parents died, I would somehow have to convince Wayne Gretzky I was worthy of adopting, because no rich American or British person adopts a Canadian baby when they seek international adoptions. If my parents died when I was young, I was basically fucked because of geography alone.

A few minutes later we got home. The hail and rain had stopped but the wind was still strong and my sister and I grabbed four baseball-size hail stones from our yard, wrapped them in tinfoil, and put them in the freezer (where we kept them for five years, so we wouldn't forget, I guess). Then my entire family sat in our basement, and while the storm passed over, we watched the destruction on CBC news.

Later that night, my mom shouted, "Kelly!" from the stairwell and she came down carrying my ruined indoor shoes. I stared at them, guiltily.

"Why weren't you wearing your outdoor shoes?"

I shrugged.

"Kelly, I can't keep buying you new stuff because you destroy it or lose it. We don't have all the money in the world!"

I shook my head. I was now mad. I had run outside in my indoor shoes to spite her. I didn't want to be left behind with the day-care ladies. Why didn't she understand that?

"I don't know," I fumed, and then, "Maybe that's what

happens when you leave your kids in a day care during tornadoes?"

I felt the flush, up my chest and neck and into my face.
I had done it.

The look crossing her face—of shock, hesitation,
acceptance—reminded me that even though I was upset
with her for doing it, I knew my mom had to leave us at day
care because she had to work and make money.

And even though I knew Mom had to nurse people and
eat smoked meats and sometimes brought home cute moc-
casins for us, I couldn't help myself. I kept going.

"We could have died today and we were all alone with
people who don't even love us." The pressure I felt in my
head from this confrontation was unbearable, like I had an
elastic band tied around my neck. My body always betrayed
me, I couldn't bluff anything.

From her side of the couch, under the soft mohair blan-
ket, Lauren raised her hand, like this was a formal talk.
"Miss Georgia *loves* me."

My mom tossed my shoes under the stairs, where old
things go to die.

"I'll go to Jack and Jill and get you new shoes. You needed
a size up anyhow." Oh, good, she's ignoring the issue at
hand. That old saw.

"And Kelly, we are all going to die someday."

I FELT SANDPAPER ON my cheek and sleepily opened my eyes
back into the real world. "Whisker burn."

It was my dad. He was rubbing his cheek on my cheek

to wake me up. Whisker burn was his nice way, with skin abrasion, of telling me it was time to get up. I put up with it, because I worried this could be my only interaction with him for the day.

"I had a bad sleep," I croaked. "I dreamed about Mom in a floating teepee and hail killing Lauren. I don't want to go to day camp ever, ever again."

"You aren't going to day camp today."

"Ever again!?"

"No, you'll have to go tomorrow. Come on, your sister is already up." He passed me peanut butter toast wrapped in a paper towel. "We're going out. You can keep your pajamas on."

My mom, dad, sister, and I piled into the Volvo station wagon and drove to the refinery on the east side of the city, where the tornado had touched down.

"I want to see this before the traffic gets too awful and it's all cleaned up." My dad almost sang the words, in a cheerful, childish way that indicated to me he was thrilled to see some destruction porn.

I sat in the backseat, my peanut-buttery, oily fingertips resting gently on the rubber along the bottom of the power windows, nose breath slightly fogging up the window. It appeared to me that a tornado was basically a vacuum without a bag, grabbing everything and spitting it out: living or not living, valuable and not valuable.

"Oh, there's a washing machine!" my dad shouted gleefully, spotting someone's top-loader washing machine on the side of the road. It was on its side, the door missing, so we could see the machine's empty insides.

"They really cleared the road fast," he shouted. "OH! OH! Look, that car is upside down! What a shame, looks like an '86."

In the midst of what was a true tragedy, my father was acting like Jacques Cousteau at his peak, coming across "treasures" right and left.

The car crept forward slowly; there were other families in cars doing the same thing we were doing, like we were all in the upside-down-world version of a drive through Safari Park. Dad kept pointing out the items off to the side of the road, or in fields, the things the tornado had dropped behind, like we weren't able to see them for ourselves. My mom looked on, often injecting "Whoa."

"Oh, that poor cow!" I saw its legs, sticking straight up like a plastic toy, then the sink on its head.

But then Dad stopped. I'm not sure if his enjoyment stopped or if he just couldn't keep up because suddenly there was everything . . . everywhere. He couldn't possibly list it all. It looked like we were in a garbage dump, but we were really in a residential area, looking at the insides of people's houses, their lives, all over the side of the road, mixed with piles of rubble. Trees left standing looked like matchsticks, branches and foliage missing from each of them.

"I watched all of this happen from my office window. It was incredible. I've never seen anything like it. Never. It's terrible. This is horrible."

Our car came to a stop; city workers were cutting a tree into pieces and throwing them into a truck.

I looked out my sister's window; she was staring at a Cabbage Patch Kid. The doll's dress was half gone, and she was caught on top of a jagged stack of Pepsi crates floating on a puddle of oily rainwater. I assume this was what prompted Lauren to start quietly crying. I mean, her Cabbage Patch Kid looked similar, and the half-nakedness of it was sort of disarming and creepy. Plus, yesterday and today were slightly traumatizing and so far she hadn't shown any sign of stress whatsoever.

"What if we'd all died yesterday?" She choked on her own snot after inhaling it to the back of her throat. "I don't want to go to day camp. I don't want to go. Kelly is right; it's stupid and it isn't even camp! I'm not going back. Never."

"This was a bad idea," Mom said. I thought maybe my parents would argue. I don't think Mom was blaming Dad for upsetting my sister, but I think he was about to take it that way.

"Lauren, Kelly understands why you go to day camp. She doesn't like it but she understands, right, Kelly?" I nodded, as Dad tried to tell her again that it wasn't his fault that she was upset.

Lauren covered her face with her hands and sucked more snot back into her head.

Mom turned around and patted her leg. Lauren began to cry more audibly, and Mom shot a look to Dad that was not reciprocated. They really dealt with drama completely differently.

"Don, I'm getting in the back."

Mom undid her seat belt and climbed between the driver's seat and the passenger's seat and sat between Lauren and me, letting Lauren crash into her.

"Lauren, what happened yesterday won't happen again. And if it does, we will have a plan, okay?"

"Yes." I nod, looking at a kitchen in a house with the wall ripped off. It looked like a really messy dollhouse. "We need a plan for natural disasters if you aren't there." That's all I really wanted.

"I'll come in with you tomorrow," Mom said.

With Lauren calming down, I looked out at a giant oil tank, moved from its spot, crushed by the natural disaster, and considered the possibility that being a parent was just as weird as being a kid. Maybe parents were faking everything and had no answers. Oh, God, that thought was terrifying. How could my creators and caregivers not know what to do? That thought lingered.

IN THE SUMMER OF 2012, my three kids, husband, and I moved to Los Angeles.

I immediately became the "annoying parent" for cutting their summer so drastically short.

"What? Mom. No. Mom? No." Sal gently shook her head back and forth. Though she was not physically demonstrating the whiny vocal angst with her lazy-looking long arms at her sides, her palms were up, pleadingly.

"School starts at the beginning of August? Mom, sixth grade at the beginning of August! That's in two weeks. How could you do this to us?"

She was right. The public schools in Los Angeles did start in August, I was cutting their summer break very, very short, and I was a terrible mother.

"Yeah, but, you live in LA now, so every day is basically summer," I squeaked out, and, not even able to believe myself, I rolled my eyes and quickly backpedaled. "Yeah, it sucks. I had no idea."

Before I moved my family to Los Angeles, I found out where the best public schools were, I made sure we had the very best health insurance; if I kept working as hard as I'd been working, I had at least five years' worth of work I could count on. I might have overlooked that school would start very early, and I'd attempted to ignore the fact that there would be earthquakes.

I guess it wasn't so much that I'd ignored the possibility of earthquakes. I'm pretty sure I was very prepared for an earthquake. But I definitely buried the notion that in this new town, this type of natural disaster was a true threat to my family. Earthquakes seemed like something I had a handle on by just buying flashlights, bags of rice, canned food, and gallons of water. Dust off my hands; I'm done. I was pretty sure that was more than most of the population in the state of California had accomplished for themselves as far as earthquake preparedness went. I put to bed in my brain the notion that California could break off and float into the ocean and I moved on with my life.

Then the first earthquake happened.

We were in our first house, on Oakdell Lane in Studio City. Gary Oldman lived in the house for years before us and I often thought about that while I lay in bed. "He looked at this same ceiling." Or, on the toilet, "He crapped on this toilet. He looked at the same wall while he crapped on this toilet." In the shower, "I bet he peed in here, too!"

These thoughts plague me in Los Angeles. Last week, I was at a friend's house, and when I complimented a gigantic, ornate bathroom door, she said, "John Malkovich put that in, he used to live here."

When I used her bathroom, I couldn't help it. I thought, *John Malkovich used to shit right here.* I'm not exactly *starstruck* by anything (except Oprah—I cried when I saw her in real life, her hair was like a lion's mane), but I am struck by the fact that famous people's poops and pees have happened while looking at the same walls I'm looking at.

The night of the first earthquake, James and I both woke up simultaneously for no reason at all. I stared at Gary Oldman's ceiling for a moment before I picked my phone up off the bedside table and saw that it was 3:15 a.m. James rolled toward me and we made eye contact in a way that wasn't sexy as much as it was confused as to why we were both awake. There had been no noise.

"Do you think a kid is up?" I whispered. "Do you think one of them is hiding at the end of the bed and is going to jump up and scare the shit out of us?"

"They aren't up." His voice was low and croaky.

I was still wondering. "Maybe it's the rats?"

There's a bizarre thing in LA, and that is canyon rats. The rats I've seen here are very cute and clean, like bunnies, only they are rats and they come out at night from the vines on the ground and the walls. Our rats, I suspected, had recently made their way into the attic and then down into the walls. I would hear their tiny teeth gnawing on something metal in the wall every night. I imagined they were trying to get into the furnace vents, and I often looked for their little cute faces behind the bars on the vents, like little jailbirds.

"Don't." James, weak with the sleeps, hit my shoulder with the back of his hand. He hated rats so much that once, when a squirrel ran by his feet too closely and too quickly, he screamed like a woman, in front of a crowd of people, and he wasn't even the slightest bit humiliated. The adrenaline pumped hard for rats.

I dropped talking about the rats with James. Both of us began to drift into unconsciousness just as it happened, our first earthquake as residents of Los Angeles.

The sound came first, like a strange south-to-north-traveling zoom. It was as though the sound was barreling through our neighborhood really fast, like a giant spaceship flying very quickly and very close to the house. First came the sound, then the movement. The bed snapped north—less than an inch, but it was a definite snap, like our bed was being launched by a mini Disneyland-ride spring, but then suddenly stopped. Then the roof really moved. Gary Oldman's ceiling creaked, snapped, and splintered much more than the bed, north and back again, moving with the zooming sound. And, as the sound of the earthquake faded away, the sounds of the terrified, furry rats on the roof turned into mayhem. It sounded like someone was rolling rats down bowling lanes up on the roof. I stared at James as we listened. Under any other circumstances I would have said it—"Rats"—but I couldn't do that to him. Not now. Instead, I moved my face closer to his, so that his beard hairs were touching my lips, and stupidly whispered the obvious. "That was an earthquake."

James and I both felt very energized by our first earthquake. We checked on the kids (they slept through it) and spent an hour repeating ourselves about that one moment, talking in circles:

"I didn't realize there would be noise!"

"Lightning has noise, why wouldn't an earthquake? The earth is moving."

"Yeah, whoa, the earth moved. We're so stupid and fragile."

"So stupid. So fragile."

"Why did we wake up right before it happened?"

"I don't know. Maybe there was a little earthquake right before that one."

"What was that? A four point five?"

I picked up my phone and googled *earthquake Los Angeles*.

"Oh, shit, no. It was only a three point seven. Oh my God. The roof would just cave in if we had a six."

"Sounded like a poltergeist going through the roof and moving the house."

"Don't tell the kids that."

I decided maybe I should get up for a pee before I fell back asleep. I sat on Gary Oldman's toilet and, looking at the ceiling he'd looked at many times before, wondered how many times that roof had scared him during earth-quakes and if he screamed like a woman when he saw rats.

I kept missing the smaller earthquakes that came after that one, but that one was very good for me. I was no lon-ger paranoid about bigger earthquakes. It was basic Psych 101 training: the more earthquakes of no consequence oc-curred, the less I cared about them. It was as if there was no longer any danger surrounding earthquakes at all. I'd post things like "So, I guess we've had eight earthquakes this week," very casually on my personal Facebook account for friends and family. (Don't try to friend me, readers, I only friend people I've hugged and made eye contact with. Facebook is the one place online that's off-limits.)

Then the second real earthquake happened.

Months and months of tiny earthquakes had passed and we'd moved to a new house on Outpost Drive, in Hollywood. The house was beautiful, a Colonial Mediterranean from the 1930s. No celebrity had ever lived there, so there were no funny throw-ups or poops to imagine, but Gary Oldman now lived up the hill from us, so I still felt a sense of home.

The noise that came from the second earthquake was deafening: I woke up shouting "EARTHQUAKE!" and couldn't even hear my own voice. The noise was so loud and the shaking violent enough that all those months of ca-sually disregarding the danger of earthquakes were tossed to the wayside as I woke up screaming, "EARTHQUAKE!" at the top of my lungs. Our cats flew off the bed like stunt-men being pulled by cables.

This quake woke up most of Los Angeles, on a Monday

morning at 6:25 a.m., in complete shock. It was the biggest asshole of an alarm clock, but at least it was set at the right time.

James mirrored my reaction, both of us alert the moment the noise and movement began. Tangled in our sheets, our reactions were the exact same, to yell "EARTHQUAKE!" and to run, tripping on duvets and decorative pillows on the floor, to get to our children.

We had once experienced something similar ten years earlier, when our door alarm chimed in the middle of the night. Not the house alarm, but the *beep-beep-beep* of the front door being opened.

Then, too, we woke up at the same time, ran, tripping on our sheets, out the bedroom and into the hall. We stopped when we saw that the door had simply been blown open slightly by the wind.

"What the fuck was our plan? What kind of badasses do we think we are?" I said, standing there, realizing that our instinct had been to run, unarmed and with one eye glued shut with sleep crust, toward a burglar.

"Speak for yourself," James said, shutting the door.

The second earthquake stopped while we were midway down the hall to the children.

"Was that an earthquake?" A tiny, scared voice came from Bea's dark room. I walked in, stifled my adrenaline-filled body, and prepared to give her a speech about how safe she was and how normal this was for Los Angeles and how everyone would be fine. "It was," I said.

"Oh, can you go now? I'm still tired."

James was in the hall, looking into Henry's room. Henry lay on his back, eyes shut, one leg under the duvet and one sticking out from the bed.

"He slept right through that."

"Jesus, what's wrong with him?"

I went to Sal's door, pushed it open slightly, and looked at Sal, her sweet head of curly hair, facing away on her pillow. "Mom? Are you *staring at me*? Yes, earthquake. Let me sleep for another forty minutes, okay? 'Bye."

I said nothing, pulling the door closed. The earthquake didn't faze my kids. But my hands were still shaking.

"That wasn't cool." I crawled back into my side of the cold bed and pressed my freezing bare legs against James's superhairy Clan of the Cave Bear legs.

"No. That wasn't cool. That was fucked up. I wonder what it was on the Richter scale." I rolled over and grabbed my phone to check my newly installed earthquake app. I downloaded it during the run of small earthquakes. I now had a bona fide, wake-up-screaming, truck-crashing-into-your-house-scale earthquake I'd survived, and . . .

"Oh my God."

"What? A six?"

"That was only a four point four."

I dropped back into my pillow, holding the phone in the air, angled to James. He took the phone with both hands as I covered my face with my own.

"James, do you know what that means?!"

"What?" He wasn't really asking what, it was a reflex "what."

I pushed my index fingers into the little inner sockets of my eyes, to feel that sting I enjoyed.

"That means if there is a *real* earthquake, we are really, really fucked. Really."

We would not be able to deal. Our kids, however, would be absolutely fine.

The morning of the second earthquake, James dropped the kids off at school while I sat on the couch, dreading my gynecologist appointment that morning. I hadn't been to the gynecologist since the birth of Beatrix, which made it approximately five years since my vagina had a health checkup.

I realize this makes me sound very neglectful of my vaginal health. It's true, I was.

The problem I had was that Bea's birth was traumatic. She didn't turn and was stuck in my vagina for quite a while. We have it on video, somewhere, I've never watched. I tried once and heard my own screaming, like a coyote crossed with a duck, and then I turned the video off. So, she, the third child and smallest of the three, ended up stuck in my vagina. After she finally dislodged, I remember a lot of blood, and a lot of cloths. Gauze. The doctor kept stuffing gauze up past my vagina and into my uterus, and I wondered, where was it all going? He was stuffing a lot in, like my uterus was a turkey . . . and it seemed like he was not pulling so much out. So, what I'm getting at is that I had a fear that the doctor who delivered Bea had left gauze in my uterus. That I had gauze up there. And if I did, I didn't really want to know.

And one year after her birth, I thought, *I can't go in now and have them find gauze up there! That's awful.*

And two years after her birth I thought, *They can't find two-year-old gauze up there! That would be so awful!*

And so on . . . Now it was year five. I was still convinced I had gauze up there, in my uterus. Things never felt right in my abdomen after having Bea. Obviously, it had to be because I had a living-taxidermy uterus.

My new gynecologist was Gene; my friend Lisa had recommended him. He was a very happy and friendly man, the kind of man who would kiss you good-bye on the mouth.

(At the end of my first appointment I texted Lisa: Does Gene kiss you on the mouth at your appointments?

Lisa: Yes. Old Jewish people do that.

Me: Okay. For a moment when I texted that to you I was worried that was a weird thing to text.)

"That earthquake was terrifying," the nurse said as I lay back on the table and put my socked feet into the stirrups.

"It was really my first biggish earthquake." The vulnerability of having my legs apart made this conversation even more uncomfortable.

"I've lived here my whole life. I've felt much bigger earthquakes," she said, "but that, that was a violent one."

Gene had entered the room. "You know, Northridge ruined me. It split my house in two. My entire pool spilled into the house. It was ruined. I moved to Malibu."

My ass was now sweating onto the white paper that usually filled me with comfort. I hated the ass cheek sweat mark of shame, but I was definitely going to leave one.

"Your house split in two?"

Gene nodded, "Yup. *Pllllt*"—he made a sound while lifting his hands in the air together and pulling them apart. "Ruined me. Most terrifying thing ever. Thank God my kids were with me when it happened."

Just then, as I sweated onto the white paper, I had a momentary blip, a vision, back to day camp with baseball-size hailstones raining down around me. Oh my God. What if I wasn't with my kids when a big earthquake happened? What if I was somewhere far away, like here, on Sunset Boulevard with a gynecologist named Gene? My mom had been with others, caretaking the sick and elderly on Native American tribal lands, when we were in a natural disaster; what if I were doing something equally honorable, just as far away, like in a meeting in Santa Monica with HBO? The two earthquakes I'd experienced so far had happened when I was with my kids.

I was so upset about not having come up with a plan for a natural disaster, when that was a such an important moment in my childhood, that I was no longer as concerned about Dr. Gene finding a gauze-stuffed turkey/uterus in my abdomen.

"Okay, we're just going to lower you. Let your knees relax." My knees were completely clamped together. I relaxed them, they popped apart, a thin layer of sweat between them. I tried to stay calm as my chair was lowered back into prone position.

"Michelle, she needs to be lowered a little more." Gene was on my right side, turning on an ultrasound machine.

"I'm trying."

"What do you mean?"

"The machine isn't working."

"What do you mean?"

"Did you unplug it over there? Maybe with your foot?" Michelle walked past my socked feet and to Gene's side of my chair. She plugged and unplugged the chair, looking confused and standing beside Gene while I lay with my vagina in the air, suddenly in the middle of some type of television comedy routine.

"There, does it work now?" he asked.

"Well, I have to go over there to check, hold on." Michelle walked past my feet again, to my left side, to get to the chair controller. Again she clicked it back and forth. "Now, Gene, are you stepping on the cord?" she asked accusingly. Neither of them seemed aware that I was sitting there, sweating a bum impression onto their white parchment paper.

"I'm not." Childlike, Gene attempted to defuse with a smile the effect of the short, hard breaths steaming out of his nostrils.

Michelle walked past my feet again, to Gene's side of my naked body, which was, you know, still mid-lowered in the exam chair, covered with a piece of paper, my socked feet in stirrups. I was a ghost in the middle of their confusion.

"You have to be stepping on it, Gene." Michelle ducked to the floor—I assumed to make sure that the connections were tight and that Gene's feet were not on them. I stared at the ceiling tiles, shifting my sweaty buttocks, wondering what celebrities had lain in that same chair and stared at the ceiling while they went through this routine.

KELLY OXFORD

"Don't move." Her hand was out, palm straight up, international sign of STOP, as she passed back to my left side.

"Okay," I said, feeling a rush of anger. I need to move my ass. I'd barely moved a muscle in the last two minutes, what the heck was her problem?

Michelle was shocked. "Oh dear, not you. I'm sorry." She picked up the controller and my chair lowered.

Gene lubed up the ultrasound wand and put it inside me. I always want to be mature about these things, I mean, this is medicine, but it's also an older man putting a dildo camera inside my vagina.

"Gene, do you see anything up there? Inside my uterus?"

"The lining is really thick."

"Oh my God, it's gauze."

"What? No." He paused and turned the screen to me. "See these?"

I looked at the black-and-white screen, shapes moving like jelly. Gene was pointing to large black circles with white rings that were coming in and out of focus, rolling around.

"Those are cysts in your ovaries. Big ones. Have you ever had one erupt? It's very painful; you would most likely go to the emergency room if it happened."

His face softened, eyes questioning; he really cared to know if one had exploded in the past. I wasn't sure why. Maybe he really was just a caring older Jewish guy who kissed on the mouth.

Then I remembered. "Oh my God. Yes. I went into the hospital in incredible pain one time on my birthday and this nurse gave me morphine and asked me to give myself an enema."

"You gave *yourself* an enema?"

"Right?! Exactly! Thank you, I was in the hospital. While high on morphine. It's really been a huge question mark in my life, like, why did that nurse ask me to do that?"

"I don't know, but you have at least ten more of those cysts in there, this one here . . ."

He showed it to me on the screen. I instantly felt like it was a thing I owned, like a dog or cat or baby. In my head I named that cyst Iris.

"This one is two inches across."

"Gross." I watched Iris bounce back and forth in my abdomen, as Gene wiggled the dildo wand around in my vagina.

"So they can just explode? At any time?"

"Yes. At any time."

I notice connections in things and events and always consider them "signs" that I should do something. Walking out of my appointment, I found my mind spinning, twisting on the undeniable link between my "could possibly blow at any moment" cyst named Iris and the possibility of the earth splitting beneath us at any moment. Everything was on shaky ground. We had to be ready. I had to do everything I could. I was in charge. I was an adult who had her shit together at all times.

Certainly, kiss-on-the-mouth Dr. Gene's discussion about being with his kids when the Northridge earthquake hit, on the day of my first scary earthquake, was a sign that I had to get myself truly prepared for an earthquake, for my kids. I needed to prevent my children from feeling the unpreparedness and fright I felt and my parents felt with the tornado in 1987. All of this connectivity made me wonder if we were just living in a video game, like Sims. Life is so mathematically repetitious. I mean, if we don't all become better people than our parents, what is the point in any of this?

I called Sal's middle school first. She was in a magnet program within a Valley public school, which had approximately two thousand students. This was my worst nightmare. Middle school was the worst anyway, because middle school kids are the worst. Puberty, peer pressure, AIDS talk. I'd had only about three hundred kids to deal with in my middle school. The fact that I put my daughter in a school with almost seven times that many jerks upset me, but it also made her a badass in my teen eyes and heart. I'd never had to deal with anything like that and it was all she knew and she was fine with it.

"Hi," I said into the receiver to the receptionist at the school. "My daughter is new at the school this year and, well, we're actually Canadians and new to Los Angeles." I paused like she'd give a shit. Rarely does anyone give a shit about immigrants. I continued, slightly defeated, "So, I can't find any information about earthquake procedure on your website. Do you have any?"

"Ma'am, sorry? What are you asking?" Confusedly, she stopped me cold and left me in that neurotic spot where I now felt the need to talk myself out of sounding like an idiot while knowingly sounding like an idiot. I paced my kitchen.

"I just, you know, since we are new here, and I can't find

any school information on the protocol if there is an earth-quake . . ." I picked up a banana and opened it as I talk and walk. Subconsciously, I guess I was trying to feel relaxed, like I was talking to a friend. I took a bite of the banana and continued. "Like, if it's a five on the Richter scale? Do we come"—I loudly swallowed some banana—"get our kids? Is it like a snow day, or not? Because where I grew up there were no snow days at all. I mean, there was just so much snow all the time we never, ever could have a snow day. Every day was a snow day. So I'm wondering if that's the same thing here, you know, but with earthquakes?" I flipped the now-empty banana peel over, in a rush of satisfaction over communicating my needs so well, stepped on the garbage lid opener, and tossed it in the garbage bin.

"Sorry, I still don't understand what you are asking about the earthquakes."

I choked, slightly, on the last bit of banana.

"Oh!" my voice obviously more urgent and less "banana chill." I was now wasting this good woman's time.

"I mean, what is the protocol for an earthquake? If it's a four, or five, or six on the scale, do we just drop everything and get our kids?"

"No," she said and stopped. I waited for her to pick the conversation back up with more information, but she did not.

"Okay. Other than that, my main question I guess is, is there a specific gate to go to, to pick up my child in the event of an earthquake?"

"Yes," she said, suddenly. As she began talking, I realized that one thing I hated the most about asking people questions is when someone doesn't just offer you the information it should be obvious that you are seeking. That they need to be asked the specific question in order to give you any information about the overall issue you are clearly getting at. It's like their brains can't make any connections whatsoever, and I really have no patience for that sort of thing, especially when I have to ask questions, which I hate doing, as I said.

"Um, then what?" I prompted her. Normally I'd just hang up in frustration, but this was life-or-death information.

"In the event of a large earthquake, parents will bring their ID to the south gate. There will be a station there and someone will check the list to make sure your child is in well-being. When the child is located on the list, and your ID verified, you will then go to the north gate to pick up your child."

I said, "Okay, great, thank you for your time," and ended the call. I repeated what she said to me in question form, to myself, rather than just asking her what she meant. "Check the list to make sure your child is in well-being"?

She could have meant . . . alive. But I was very certain she did mean dead. I mean, they have a list of students they need to account for if there is a large earthquake and presumably the building could fall apart and hurt some kids. I decided to save that for later discussion, or obsession.

I was already dialing Henry's school.

"Hi, I'm a parent at the school and I'd like to speak to someone there about earthquake procedure."

"That's me!"

"Great, so this is our first year in the school, we moved from Canada—"

"Oh! How are you liking it?" This one cared. Thank God.

"It's better than freezing. Look, I am not sure what the rules are for earthquakes and the kids in school. Do we come for something over a five on the scale? And what gate—"

This was where the woman cut me off, very excitedly, and rolled into a monologue of epic proportions.

"I just want to assure you that we have everything under control at this school and you will have very little to worry about in the event of an earthquake. Our school takes time every month to go through proper earthquake responsiveness with the children. They are very conditioned to respond quickly and safely during an event.

"We are very proactive in our preparedness. The school has two weeks' worth of fresh water in a tank, to be used only in the case of an emergency, such as that. It is enough water for every single student. That's fresh water access for one thousand children; it's a lot! We also change the water tank out monthly, which is great. Of course, we also have prepackaged food for all children; they will get three meals a day. Ummmm, what else . . . Oh! Of course, the kids won't be allowed in the buildings after an earthquake, you know they're really old buildings, so the tents are all on campus and they will sleep eight children and two adults. And we have beds and pillows. As far as security goes, all gates will be locked down and we will have our armed security on the grounds at all times. We teachers and staff do not leave the campus until all of the children are placed and parents have one week to pick up their kids and if they don't make the one-week cutoff, for whatever reason, the children will be turned over to the state. Thankfully, we are a school that is prepared and optimistic." She giggled, earnestly. "I hope that covered it all. Is that enough of an answer for you?"

I was barely breathing by this point. "Actually," I whispered, "I was just wondering what gate I could pick him up at."

This was the opposite of the conversation with Sal's school. Instead of getting no answer at all, I got much, much more than I'd ever imagined. Everything I never wanted to know, including the answer to the one question I did have.

"Oh," she said. "East gate."

When James came home with the kids, I pulled him into the bedroom, shut the door on the kids, and grabbed both sides of his beard, staring into his eyes.

"We need to leave and go back to Canada, where the only danger is the cold and a tornado every seventy-five years."

"Why?"

"An earthquake could kill us. An earthquake could kill us while the kids are in school and then the kids will sit there for a week in tents until they are turned over to the state in some sort of Hurricane Katrina, Superdome situation."

"That won't happen."

"It could."

"It won't."

"James, we have one kid in the Valley, one kid in Hollywood, and one that's at home. If there is an earthquake, we need a plan. Our cell phones won't work, who will get which kid? We need running shoes in our car trunks. We won't be able to drive anywhere. Think of the mayhem of cars if there was an earthquake during the day! We will all have to walk. Oh, God, if I'm on the other side of the hills I'll have to cross mountains to get home. By foot. James. This place is a fucking death trap."

"Kelly. It won't happen. It could, but it won't."

"Today I found out I have a belly full of cysts that could burst at any moment and cause me so much pain I need to go to the ER. Remember when I gave myself an enema at the hospital? When I was high on morphine?"

"Yes."

"Well, that was a cyst."

"Wait, what?"

"It's the same thing, James. The cysts and the earthquakes. I don't think my mom really thought there was a chance a tornado like that could come through our city. She had an excuse for not having a plan. I don't. James, we can leave. We can leave the earthquakes and schools that collect two weeks' worth of water but still turn your kids over to the government if you're a week behind and we could go back to Canada. I can't run from this belly."

I was clearly spiraling.

"We aren't leaving; you're just scared. Tell me everything and let's come up with a plan."

I told James about the tents, gates, food, lists, ID, everything.

He stopped me. "Okay, that sounds great and everything, but I meant your ovarian cysts. What are we doing about those?"

I shook my head and wandered from the room. "Nothing, those just happen when they want to happen. Just like the earthquakes."

I pushed Sal's bedroom door open. She was sitting up in her bed, expressionless, watching a movie on her laptop. When she saw me, she pulled the earbud from her right ear and let it drop to the bed, but her expressionless face remained unchanged.

"Yeah?"

"I just wanted to see if you needed anything. Water? You stressed? Everything okay in your life? I mean, I don't want you to be stressed. You stressed?"

"Water is good, thanks," Sal said, still emotionless, but she hadn't put the earbud back in her ear, so my existence was noted in her way.

"I have cysts."

"Gross."

"Okay. I'll grab that water for you. I just don't want you to be stressed about anything. I came up with a plan for earthquakes." I was talking like an idiot and she was already an expert bullshit detector.

"Mom, I'm not stressed, you are."

"When I was a kid I really wanted to go to summer camp and my mom sent me to day camp, but really it was day care. Anyhow, then there was a tornado and she wasn't around and we didn't have a family plan and it really freaked me out. So I just wanted to have a plan. For us. So that wouldn't happen to you."

"I want to go to summer camp."

"It's like two thousand dollars per kid for one week, we can't. Not this year."

I got to her door and turned around before she jammed the sound plug back into her sweaty, teen ear hole.

"Sal, if there's a really big earthquake while you're home, you know you stand right here."

I pushed my hands against both sides of the door frame and pretended I was in a big earthquake. I held on tight and rocked back and forth, standing directly across the room from her bed, where the light on the laptop reflected on her face. "Just stand right here and hold on and everything will be fine." She said nothing, and in the silence, no longer thrashing but still holding the door frame, I nodded. She stared at me and slowly adjusted the earbud she'd just inserted.

"Mom, you're really weird. And you're totally wrong; you go under the table. You always go under a table. You never go into a doorway."

Really?

"Right. Right. I was just testing you."

She stared at me blankly. I wondered if she was wondering how on earth she could have such an impossibly stupid mother and survive day-to-day. I wondered if she had already had the realization that parents don't have all the answers to everything. I wondered if she was or would ever be as stressed as I was.

"I'll grab you that water."

No Real Danger

In 1998 I noticed I had sore armpits. They felt more achy than bruised, which seemed strange because what is true now was true then: I don't move a lot. There is no exercise, there is no heavy lifting, sports, or stretching. And the soreness was not related to odd lumps or my glands, because that is medical 101 and would have sent off alarms to visit my doctor immediately, so I let it be. After ignoring several months of the pain, I stood facing the mirror one afternoon and looked closely at my armpits as I shaved. I could not figure them out. Where was the pain starting and ending? Confused, I went to visit my family doctor, Dr. Cotton.

Because my mother was a hypochondriac, Dr. Cotton saw me a lot. I say a lot, but I could use words like "the most," or "Every time I left the house it was either school or the doctor," and it wouldn't be hyperbole. On average my mom would take me in twice a week. I had backstories for all of the Kodak babies on Dr. Cotton's walls and in the second grade I listed "banana-flavored antibiotics" as my favorite drink. A lot.

"Lie down," Dr. Cotton said gently. The familiar sound of the crinkly white paper instantly relaxed me. "What have you been up to?" she asked. "Still working at your dad's office?"

"Yeah." I stared into the Chinese Kodak baby's face. I'd decided, when I was very young, that he was the genius baby because that stereotype was real. Matthew Wong was the smartest kid in all my classes. This Chinese Kodak baby was the one that smiled first and had the best heart. He was so much nicer than the little blond baby who liked to pinch. "I just went on tour with my boyfriend's band. It was pretty boring. Nothing too new."

"Is this the same guy you were with in the summer?" she asks, as she dries her hands at the sink.

"I was dating another guy this summer I think. I don't know."

"Okay, where is the problem."

I lifted my arm and pointed into the pit. "It's really sore, right here. It's been like this for a week, maybe a few weeks. I may have initially noticed it a few months ago. I can't take it anymore. I don't feel a lump but I'm fully prepared to biopsy."

Dr. Cotton was the doctor I went to when I was eleven and found a lump under my nipple. She examined me, then informed me very professionally that the lump I was feeling was actually just my boob. Growing. Dr. Cotton was a magical doctor who seemed to turn all of my terrifying ailments into nothing of concern. Surely she could turn this sore armpit into some news as wonderful as boobs.

"You worry a lot, right, Kelly?" she inquired as she pushed on the sore spot. I winced. "Ow—yes. But nothing out of the ordinary. I think I'm pretty normal because you know, who doesn't worry? Dead people, that's who. I'm actually a very, very chill person."

She gently lowered my arm back to the table and gave my leg a pat. "You can get up." I sat up and felt weird shame as she washed my armpit sweat off her fingers at her little doctor's sink. Like, shouldn't she be chill about my armpit? Under that sink were tongue depressors and throat-swabby things. When I was eight, I'd stolen several thousand of those long Q-Tip strep-throat things from under that sink, you know, to practice swabbing my throat at home, to rid myself of the gag it caused. To this day, doctors are impressed with the motionlessness I have mastered during a strep swab. That's how chill I was. I wasn't neurotic at all. Every child practices throat swabbing in the privacy of their basement bathroom with the hanging lightbulb. It's common courtesy not to gag. I could control my gag.

"So, did I just pull a muscle or something? Like maybe when I was washing my hair in the shower? Or sharply turning my steering wheel?" I asked, hopefully.

"Kelly," she started as she dried off her hands, "have you heard of panic disorder, or panic attacks?"

The blood drained from my face, my arms got sweaty, my ears began ringing. I felt like I'd been insulted.

"Whoa, no, no . . ." I threw my hands in the air.

"They're very common. I see kids your age, right out of high school, who come in here with panic disorder all the time. It's very common. Let's do some blood work to be sure there isn't anything else going on, but I'm pretty sure you've had panic disorder since you were twelve."

"And you're just telling me now?" I exclaimed, keeping my emotion sounding like a three when I was really feeling a nine, like a totally emotionally stable person.

"Well, I wasn't going to suggest you were eventually going to get panic disorder if you weren't."

"Dr. Cotton, do you think all of my obsessively frequent doctor's visits set me up for a lifetime of general worry?"

"I don't think anything caused this necessarily, it's involuntary. With panic disorder the body just reacts to stimulus differently, adrenaline mostly. Mundane things become fight or flight."

I hop off the table. My arms are aching more, my ears are ringing; and I feel light-headed; flight feels good right now.

"Okay. So will the armpit thing go away?"

"This is completely manageable. I see it all the time."

Yeah, she didn't answer me. This means it is an incurable situation. I'd always hoped for some disease in my life, to add some morose glamour. Like when I got mono in the fifth grade and wrote to Kirk Cameron to tell him about my "kissing disease," hoping he'd find it evocative of me to have at such a young age. I took a lab sheet and a referral for a therapist from her hands and fled the office. I didn't even say good-bye to Denise at the front desk, which is re-markable because I'd always said good-bye to her . . . every few days for the past twenty years.

I drove the three blocks from Dr. Cotton's office to the lab, pulled into the parking lot, and let my eyes soft-focus on the traffic around me. I was confused. I didn't feel panic. Not in the sense that I wanted to run, or scream, but when she said it, it clicked. I was stressed about everything. I was twenty, not going to university because I didn't want to be-come a teacher, doctor, lawyer, or engineer, and I was very, very stressed about my future. This was stress-related.

This is it, I thought. This is my great illness. This is the reason I've been going to the doctor my whole life. I began to cry, and tried to find a silver lining. Nothing, nothing, oh . . . well, at least I have something new to define myself, I thought. "Panic disorder" seemed somewhat glamorous. Not as glamorous as the kissing disease, but still maybe, I don't know . . . cute? Relatable? Then I got it, I wasn't Jew-ish, but apart from officially converting this was as close to Jewish as I could get. There, silver lining.

I shoved the lab sheet into my pocket, wiped my eyes,

KELLY OXFORD

and headed into the lab to get blood work that would eventually return completely normal.

AFTER A MOMENT OF researching panic attacks online (it really was only a moment, there were only two links and a flash page with information because it was 1998), I decided that I'd never had one. I'd never felt my heart pounding out of my chest, unless I was running (which I hadn't done since childhood). I'd never felt like I was dying or going crazy. Sure, I worried a lot and had sore armpits, but those weren't panic attacks. I decided that I wouldn't tell anyone about the outcome of my visit with Dr. Cotton. I hadn't had a panic attack yet, so what was the point? I would just embarrass myself, no one cared about sore armpits. Maybe my stress was the same as everyone else's stress. Other people worried about AIDS and kidnapping and getting uncontrollable fungal infections or yeast in their ears during the summer swimming season. There was no formal panic test given so, who knew? I was probably just plain old neurotic.

I logged off the modem and walked upstairs.

"What did Doctor Cotton say today?" My mom was cutting onions and crying. I think this is what Ukrainians do, for 70 percent of their lives.

"Oh, nothing really. She was like, huh, I don't know, so I went and got some lab work done."

She wiped her face with her sweater. "Great. Want to hear about yoga?"

"No."

"Did Doctor Cotton say anything else?"

"She said she thought I was stressed."

Mom stopped cutting onions; the room was cold enough and the tears were flowing so warmly that her glasses were fogged up. She put down the knife. I tried not to look worried.

"Oh yeah?" She pulled the glasses down and looked over them. "What are you stressed about? Anything I can help with?"

I couldn't make eye contact. I looked at the kitchen cabinets, shook my head, shrugging my shoulders trying to look casual. "I don't know, she's probably wrong. I don't get it. Those smell good."

"Pierogi." She smiled and began to chop onions again. I walked out of the room.

"What do you want for dinner tomorrow?" she called to me. My mother always asked what I wanted for dinner, ridiculously ahead of schedule, and I always replied the same:

"Whatever."

AT MY BOYFRIEND'S GIG that night, I was standing against the bar, holding my arm in the air and massaging my left armpit, when a frat jock stranger asked what I was doing. "Oh, this?" I pointed to my armpit. He nodded. "Not much, my armpits are sore. I'm also trying to figure out what I'm stressed about because apparently it could be really fucking with me." His eyebrows flew up as he made that falling sound whistle and walked away.

"Hey! Kelly!" One of the bartenders, Joan, leaned toward me, shaking her head. Joan was Indian and articulated every word; this made her seem one hundred times more knowledgeable than anyone else we knew.

"You didn't have to talk to that guy," she said. "You don't owe anyone an explanation."

I thought about that for, like, half a second. "What?"

She explained this simple concept to me again, but slower: "When someone asks you a question, it doesn't mean you have to answer. You don't owe anyone anything."

What? Wait. Really? That guy who just asked me what I was doing—I could have ignored him? Did I always just give people what they asked for? Why was I talking to strangers and why had this concept of not giving them an answer when I don't feel like it never occurred to me? What? "You mean that jock guy?"

Joan sighed and eyeballed the band. "Are you still dating Reed?" I nodded. Her grimace marked her disapproval. "He's really young." He was twenty-six, she was twenty-six, I was twenty. She laughed. "Look at him. He's a *boy*." I looked at Reed onstage; he seemed cute but she said *boy* in such an evocative way. "Kelly, you need to date a man. Someone educated and wise. Stop dating these loser boys who aren't doing anything with their lives."

Joan's wisdom was coming at a time when I needed guidance the most, and maybe she was right. Maybe all of these sweet guys with tattoos, and bands, with drug dealer roommates weren't for me. Why *was* I picking guys that were technically much older than me, but mentally a lot younger than me? I was really happy Joan had pointed out that I had options beyond the guys with tattoos in bands that I'd been dating since high school, which, by the way, was three years ago. I was quickly beginning to believe it possible that my life would improve once I stopped dating these . . . boys? I decided to dump Reed, right after the show. There was no way I'd be so stressed if I had a real man in my life. No more baby men for me. Suddenly my armpits felt lighter.

Joan touched my shoulder. "Hey, Ben's here. Can you tell him I'm in the back cashing out?" Ben was Joan's closest male friend. He looked like Ross from *Friends*, and just like Ross, he had a Ph.D. and was a part-time professor. Unlike Ross, he worked at not one, but three of the fanciest restaurants in the city. Ben said hello and I grabbed his face and stuck my tongue down his throat. That's how you let a man know he's dealing with a real woman.

The first few weeks of dating Ben were just what my armpits and worries about my impending future needed. My armpits loved that he had a newly leased car that never had to be jump-started, they loved that he lived in a rented house and not an apartment, but most of all my armpits loved that Ben did his own laundry in his own washing machine and his clothing never smelled like that damp mildew clothing.

I totally forgot about Dr. Cotton and the panic disorder. Joan was right—I mean, look, she totally hated me for listening so closely to her advice and taking her best friend away from her—but she was right. Ben was the man I needed. I was even happier working at my dad's small office downtown.

Ben introduced me to people as his "lovely girlfriend"

who'd introduced him to "the realities of sexual harassment and catcalling." He took me to fancy dinners and held my hand across the table. He taught me tons of new things about sex, things I didn't even know humans did. Strangers were so entirely struck by our matureness that they would stop what they were doing and tell us things like, "What a nice couple you two are!" and "It's so nice to see young love." These were things that a girl NEVER heard when she was dating a boy who had seventeen skulls tattooed on his neck and the base of his skull. Your armpits were always sore when your boyfriend's wallet was attached to a chain and there was never any money in it. I learned very quickly that I never had to worry about my future while-I-was-playing-the-role-of-a-normal-middle-class-white-person-grown-up.

AFTER WE HAD BEEN dating for a month, Ben brought me to meet his mother. As we pulled up the driveway of her beautiful house on the nice side of the valley, he gave me a "heads-up" type of prologue: "Okay, so my dad left my mom about a month ago because he's gay and my mom—you'll like her, she's very sweet—but because of that she's now crazy. She gets panic attacks. It's pathetic."

"Panic attacks are totally pathetic." I force laughed, my right hand shooting into my left armpit on pure reflex. Despite my rejection of the panic disorder diagnosis, I couldn't help but feel slightly wounded at the dismissal of panic as "pathetic."

Ben took my hand. "You're the nicest girl I've ever brought to meet my mom." Silver Lining.

Ben's mom and I hit it off over iced teas in her backyard. How could I not fall in love with a woman who'd had sex with a gay man her whole life? We petted her corgis and discussed squirrels, *Cosmo*, *General Hospital*, and life while Ben stayed quiet in the hammock. I was a total hit as a girlfriend.

The corgi talk, laughs, and iced teas with the mom, if there was any lingering doubt about my evolution as a human being, it really just went out the door at that moment. I was a woman. The next afternoon, as I finished up my filing, I called Ben. He sounded strange.

"Can you meet me at the Sugarbowl?"

I walked into the coffeehouse and spotted Ben's fro immediately. But beneath his studious shearling and plaid scarf he looked grim.

"Kelly." He leaned into the table. I took his hand but he didn't close his fingers around mine. I took it again, like, a do-over, but his fingers were dead. I stared at his open hand, with my desperate one around it, guessing what was coming.

"I don't think this is going to work."

My armpits rang.

"Well." He sat back, pulling his hand slowly out of mine. Oh God. He took his hand away. That's it, it's gone. We're done.

"Yesterday, while you were talking about your life to my mom, I couldn't help thinking. You just graduated high school and you really haven't done . . . anything. What do you want to do? I mean, do you have any goals? I can tell you really like corgis, but, you just work at your dad's office and stay up on your computer at night." The soreness had turned into pain, and was ripping through my side. Should I tell him I wanted to be a screenwriter and on those late nights I was trying to perfect the art of dialogue, or did that sound flaky? I had no idea who I was and that was translating as sore armpits.

"I'm pretty happy," I whispered unconvincingly as I grabbed the water that was on the table with my orphaned hand. The hand began shaking uncontrollably as I lifted the glass from the table. My hand was definitely a seven on the Richter scale. I put the glass down, hoping he hadn't seen the trembling. I wasn't really thirsty anyway. Silver lining. I breathed.

He continued, "Look. I have a Ph.D. A *P. H. D.* And you, Kelly, are a very pretty girl and you're funny and you're a high school graduate who files papers and goes to bars every night." I was suddenly wanting, yearning to tell him how much the giant hairy mole on his back disgusted me, and how I was pretty sure it was cancerous.

Ben forged on, "You're a really great girl. I mean, you're really, really great. And I can't believe I'm dumping you. But I have to. I need to date someone who has a real life. A woman, you know? I mean, I have a Ph.D."

By the time I pulled away from the parking meter, my vision was blurry. My body felt strange, electrified yet numb. I was suddenly so suspicious of everything and everyone. Had Joan given Ben the Reed speech, but about me? I felt like everyone on the street was looking at me strangely and yet I wasn't looking around at the people to be able to make that call. I didn't feel like I was in my body anymore at all when a giant Safeway truck began to pull into my lane and I hit the curb, slamming on the brakes, coming to a stop with one wheel up on the sidewalk. Cars were honking. My heart was pounding. I began to cry.

I felt officially crazy. Nothing felt normal or real. I shook and shook and somehow blindly drove myself home, following the lane line in the middle of the road.

I opened the side door and called out a hello into the house but no one was home. When I reached the top of the stairs, I instantly felt panic. Like from the very pit of my soul I felt I was worthless and everyone knew it and I would never ever climb out and feel better. That even if I did climb out, it would still be as terrible as it felt right at that moment. I felt like I was jailed inside my own sick body and my body was definitely going to kill me. I did note that I was not feeling suicidal, which was a relief, but not a silver lining because I was standing there, feeling like death and wondering if suicide would come next. Somehow it didn't enter my mind. My mind was my punishment. I looked into my bedroom. It was a mess, clothing everywhere. I still had a Cure poster on the wall, for Christ's sake. I was a disaster. Pathetic. I felt like I'd lost my mind completely and that's when I realized: this was a panic attack.

I felt vomit rising and just barely made it to the toilet in time. Now I had lost my mind *and* I was throwing up. I threw up until my throat was sore. Every time I tried to go into my bedroom to lie down, I would throw up. I was throwing up bile and blood. I was throwing up at the sight of my own room. I couldn't stop the feelings and I couldn't stop the sickness. My mind was spinning, spiraling, I couldn't stop moving. I couldn't lie still. I was rubbing my leg, my arms, pacing and rocking. I felt trapped in my body and was unable to relax. I wasn't sure how much time went by until I looked at the clock; it had been an hour, and I suddenly realized that no one would be home until my mom was done teaching yoga at eight o'clock that night. The irony of me needing yoga, my mom teaching her class a few blocks away, and me hating it so much was not blind to me. There was no way this could go on for three more hours. I would rather be dead.

I picked up the phone and called my friend Angela, who was working at the video store. "I am freaking out. I can't stop throwing up. It's the anxiety. It's a panic attack. I want to die, but I'm not, like suicidal."

"Oh my God! Don't kill yourself!" she screamed into the phone, then I heard the phone muffle as she covered the mouthpiece and said, "It's fine, she's fine," to someone in the store.

"Angela? I'm not suicidal, I just want this to end."

"Tell me everything that is happening." Angela loved dramas and that's part of why I loved her so much.

"Ben dumped me because I'm a loser and then I was almost killed by a Safeway truck."

"Kelly, Ben is a loser. A huge fucking loser. I didn't want to tell you, but—"

"He has a Ph.D., and is half *a professor*," I interrupted.

"BUT HE ISN'T AND IT DOESN'T COUNT. HE IS

A LOSER. Who has three waiter jobs if they're a real doctor of anything? Besides, you need to look after yourself and figure out what you want. You can't hide behind a dude."

"Angela, I get it. I do. I think I'm going crazy. I feel totally crazy. Nothing feels real. I am terrified and throwing up every time I look at my bedroom. I'm throwing up so hard my stomach started to bleed. That isn't cool! I can't-stop-moving. I can't even drive myself to see Doctor Cotton. I almost died because I have sore armpits and now I throw up when I look in my bedroom!"

Angela told me to count things and lie down.

So I did.

For a week.

For a week my mom brought me onion-based foods and told me I would be fine, even when I finally admitted to her that Dr. Cotton had told me I had anxiety disorder. This was the woman who had once brought me to the doctor when she found a gray hair in my eyebrow. Her nonreaction to what was occurring to me made me feel slightly more powerful, which I believe was her intent, but what was very fleeting soon only made everything feel more surreal. Days and nights blurred into each other, because I couldn't sleep unless I was passing out from exhaustion. I was crazy and specifically told my mom that she should commit me because the sight of my own bedroom made me feel like I was about to vomit. And the few times I did lie in my own room I would vomit. But she did not commit me. Suddenly I was more available to her than ever. In the past, when she wanted to "talk" or have "girl time" I had run out the door, but now I was a captive audience. Apart from her daughter asking her to commit her to a psych ward, this was a mother's dream. I couldn't go anywhere. It was like that movie *Misery*, only more endearing, really. For a week, my mother cooed and told me I'd be fine and fed me, then she'd ask me for advice on outfits and tell me gossip about her yoga friends, as I lay in her bed, in my own personal hell, wondering when I would snap out of it, but also kind of loving just being a talking head with my mother.

On day eight, I realized no one had called for me and I wasn't snapping out of anything. My dad didn't care if I showed up to work to file and make coffee. I realized I could be dead and no one would give a shit. My life meant nothing.

On day nine, I stopped talking.

On day ten, my mom took me to see Dr. Cotton. She waited in the car.

"Kelly, what's going on?" Dr. Cotton liked to start conversations before she even entered the room. Her voice was so calm and so loud at the same time.

"Panic attack," I said as she closed the door.

"When?"

"The last ten days. Now."

Her mouth dropped. I nodded, feeling numb to the embarrassment. "I can't look in my bedroom without throwing up. I feel like I'm drugged, and my mom has had me hostage for a week while she told me about yoga and swamis and home decorating shows and asks me to rate her outfits. I love her, but enough is enough." Dr. Cotton opened the door, walked down the hall, then quickly returned holding a small white pill. "Your mom was a nurse on a psych ward, there's no way she sees you as ill. You're her capable daughter and she's seen the worst. Take this Ativan. Under your tongue."

I would have taken anything. I put the pill under my tongue and felt the bitter graininess dissolve.

"Now breathe with me." I took several deep breaths along with Dr. Cotton. I stared into the eyes of all the Kodak baby photos hanging on her wall and noticed something. "Where is the Chinese baby?" She'd replaced him with a stupid motivational slogan: Mistakes Are Proof That You're Trying.

She laughed. "I retired him. He's in the closet. You know, he's probably twenty years old now." Suddenly, whatever had been holding on to me was gone. I relaxed. The vice grip that had been on my body, that slowly grew from my armpits to my stomach, body, and brain, had been released. I felt like I was awake and yet also in a deep sleep. I said good-bye to Denise and carried the photo of the Kodak Chinese baby, the one who smiled first, before all the other Kodak babies, the one with the good heart, to my mom's car.

That night, I entered my room without vomiting and firmly shut the door on my mom. After all of that time without control, I suddenly felt like I had a do-over. A new lease on life. I decided on some long-term goals.

1. Don't date until you respect yourself and know your worth.
2. Find a new job.

KELLY OXFORD

3. Get a haircut.
4. Work on being chill.
5. Spend more time with my mom.
6. Move out.
7. You don't owe anybody anything.

I decided to start at the top of the list and work down. I applied for a job at the most notoriously elitist independent clothing boutique in Edmonton. They would never hire a crazy person who had no goals or drive. I wanted to prove my worth, as a chill woman with a high school diploma.

Their five-part interview process included a half-hour presentation on the next season's trends. I got the job by bullshitting about the color orange and repeating dialogue from the magazine scene in *Funny Face*. When I was told that out of twenty applicants, I had been selected, I was triumphant, even if it was just a city of just under one million people, even if it was just Edmonton.

On my first day at work, as I struggled to fold $400 jeans, a woman approached me, smiling. It was Ben's mother.

"I'm so happy to see you again," she said, touching my arm. "I like your hair short like this." I smiled, I was happy to see her, too.

"How are you doing?" I asked.

"I'm well. Jerry is still a cocksucker." I laughed. "So sorry things didn't work out with you and Ben."

I nodded, "Oh no. It's fine. Our relationship proved very helpful for me in general." Silver lining.

She smiled as she began to leave. "I'll tell Ben I saw you and you looked great."

"Thanks," I replied. "You can also tell him I'm really chill and he's an asshole with a cancerous mole."

"Will do," she laughed, "will do."

I went home that night, able to enter my own bedroom again without vomiting blood. I crawled under my duvet, smelling of Mom's dinner, underneath the watchful eye of the Chinese Kodak baby, who'd replaced the Cure poster.

Be the Village

I have Aiden, Henry's preschool classmate, at my house. The only reason this is happening is that his mother took the initiative and had Henry over to their house first, so obviously I owe her. I would never have taken the initiative. I rarely speak to other parents at the school; other parents are strangers. I barely have time for the friends I already have and love. I don't need the pressure of new friends. No new friends. I'm sorry, I know you're amazing, it's me—I'm weird. Thanks, but no thanks. Unfortunately, children need friends.

I mean, so I have been told.

By my children.

"Playdates" are basically two parents agreeing to *be the village.*

Ideally, it goes something like this:

> **TOM'S MOM:** "Hi, Joe's mom. My son Tom asked if your son Joe could come over after school and stay through dinner, would that be okay with you? Does he eat gluten?"
>
> **TRANSLATION:** "Crap, I forgot your name. Look, I'd hoped you'd invite Tom over first, but since you haven't, I'm going to have your kid over first to get this 'it takes a village to raise a child' shit rolling, then you owe me. Does he eat gluten?"
>
> **JOE'S MOM HEARS:** "Hi, I don't know your name. Would you like to drop your son Joe off at school at 8 a.m. and not have to deal with him again until 6:30 p.m.? Of course, this means that at some point Tom has to hang out with you at your place for the same amount of time and maybe do a sleepover. Also, does he eat gluten?"

Unless the inviting family is suspicious, there is a previous appointment, or a high-level threat of terrorism is expected that day, the answer to a playdate invite will always be "Yes." And so, with the anticipation of ridding yourself of your child for a few hours where he or she will have *"wayyyyyyy more fun than we ever have at our house!"* the deal is sealed.

"Hey, Aiden, want to go in the backyard?" Henry yells this question in Aiden's general direction as he pulls packets of string cheese from the fridge with the perpetually sweaty, dirt-layered hands every five-year-old seems to possess.

Henry yells everything he wants to communicate. Because of this, we had his hearing checked earlier this year, and it turned out he wasn't hard of hearing, he's just a bit of an asshole. I help the boys into their toques (America: A toque is a woolen hat) and open their string cheese. They drop the plastic wrappers on the floor and sprint for the backyard. This simple act of assholery makes me long for childhood again. Being a child is a magical time, where you can drop your garbage on the floor and it magically vanishes. "Hey, Henry!" I yell to Henry. "One day you'll be twenty-three, you're going to stick an apple sticker to the side of the sink, look at it, and realize, you're gonna have to peel that off and put it in the garbage yourself."

Henry stops, looks at me, and rubs his nose.

"OH, NEVER MIND!"

I monitor the boys from where I sit on my butt on the carpet beside the sliding doors that lead to the yard, listening through the window to them talking.

"She's over here. We had her for two years. She bit through my finger one time when she thought it was a corn kernel. Then we put her in the ground."

All true. I feel a warm sense of pride, listening to Henry

tell his friend Aiden the high highs and low lows of having a pet hamster.

We recently found her body stiff in the cage, in the furnace room, where we kept her at night because she was so fucking loud. I didn't realize they were nocturnal. God bless any child who sleeps with a hamster in their room; they must have terrible rodent-sound-fueled nightmares.

We held a little funeral ceremony for Penelope, our hamster. Some maudlin Sarah McLachlan playing, and Penelope's body stuffed into a toilet paper roll casket.

"She's under that giant rock!" Henry stated emphatically. He was pointing at the wrong rock, but Christopher Columbus mistook America for India, and America still gave him his own holiday, so I let him be.

Henry runs to the rock. "Come on!" he yells to Aiden, who jogs up to Henry. They both stand over the rock for a moment, their foggy breath coming out in panted puffs of cloud. Henry grabs the rock and begins to pull it over.

"No!" Aiden cries, suddenly coming to a realization.

"Don't pull the rock off! I don't want to see a dead hamster. I DON'T WANT TO SEE YOUR DEAD HAMSTER!"

I can see the sudden terror enter Henry's eyes. Both boys quickly switch to the other side of the rock, trying to hold it upright. *"Pull, pull!"* they yell as they try to get the rock back up, trying to keep it from uncovering the dead hamster. They scream in their shrill little-girl voices. It isn't even a sound that comes from their throats; it's more like the highest pitch a human can make. Aiden's mouth is open as wide as it can open, his eyes clenched shut as he holds on to that rock like he's in a barrel going over Niagara Falls.

I then remember I'm the only adult present, throw my boots on, open the sliding glass doors, and run over to them in the garden. I put my hand on the top of the dead hamster rock. "Guys, stop! Stop yelling! This isn't even the right rock, the dead hamster rock is that one over there."

"Dead hamsters are scary!" Aiden shrieks.

"Why did we put her inside of a toilet roll?!" Henry squeals.

"Because she fit in there!" It made sense at the time.

I needed to switch gears; the last thing I needed was for Aiden to ask to call his mom and for me to be labeled the "mom who allowed her son to dig up a pet cemetery on a playdate" for the next six school years. "Does anyone here want lunch?"

"ME!!!" Both boys turn and face each other, smiling, their eyes locked, and hands in the air. They are just at the age where they understand social cues, and their egos can't handle how delighted they are with themselves over it. A few months ago they barely noticed a friend was in the room, and now, the act of simultaneously raising their hands in the air and shouting "ME!!!" makes them feel like geniuses. Like two billionaires sneaking glances as they do some insider trading, these boys think they're really the shit.

"Great! Let's have macaroni and cheese," I suggest.

"Ewwwwww!" Henry yells. "I hate macaroni and cheese, it smells like barf."

Some moments in parenthood become so paralyzing and tedious that no matter how brief they are, no matter how much you love your child, the repetition wears you out. This repetition doesn't last days, or weeks, it lasts years.

Seven weeks after your first child is born is around the time when you're sitting alone with your almost-two-month-old newborn, changing his diaper for possibly the one thousandth time already, and your hand stops moving as you stick the tab to the front of the diaper because it has hit you. "Oh . . . so, this isn't going to stop."

Because—believe it or not, no matter how prepared or smart you are as a human being—for a while, after you have your first baby, you're thinking, "Okay, I'm just going to get through this rough part. Things definitely have to change for a while, man, I'm working really hard, but I'm getting through it! I'm doing it! I'm really great at all of this stuff."

And then, somewhere around week seven or eight, you realize this is your new life.

This level of work isn't going to change, you are now a parent and this is just the way things are going to be. This feeling of responsibility, this "putting someone ahead of your own needs" situation, is just not going to go away. And it truly is that repetition, day in and day out, that wears you down. And so a moment, a moment as tiny as your macaroni and cheese–eating son suddenly deciding he thinks mac and cheese tastes like barf? Thus throwing the entire lunch-feeding dynamic you have created totally out of whack and necessitating a new strategy? That sets you back, that gives you gray hairs. What on earth will possibly replace mac and cheese? God damn it, Rome is crumbling before you when suddenly, a tiny voice pipes up, "Henry's mom? Can we go to McDonald's? My mom lets me eat there!"

My shoulders drop a full two inches and I'm thankful there isn't an adult there to register how much the mention of McDonald's relaxes me. "Yes, we can. And call me Kelly. Come over anytime. You're my favorite friend."

"I WANT A HAMBURGER with ketchup and cheese, please!" Henry yells from the backseat.

"You mean, a cheeseburger with ketchup?" I correct.

"Nooooo, a hamburger with ketchup and cheese, please!"

"Got it. Aiden? What about you? You're sure you can eat here?"

"Yes, I always get the cheeseburger Happy Meal."

"Got it." I figure I'm covered. If he's lying and his mom is mad I've brought him here, she can be mad because her kid is a dirty little liar, not because I brought them to McDonald's. Besides, I'm the monster for getting them sliced apples instead of fries.

We're in the drive-through line. Drive-throughs are an institution in Canada, where the weather can actually kill you. Sometimes, sitting up in the front seat, knowing your kids are strapped to a seat behind you, immovable, is liberating and having a face-to-face conversation with a cashier at a drive-through window without someone with tiny little hands grabbing at your inner thigh can be exhilarating.

"Hello, welcome to McDonald's, how may I help you this afternoon?"

"Hi! Can I get two cheeseburger Happy Meals, one with only ketchup, and sliced apples?"

"MOM!"

"Shh. And one McChicken and one small fry."

"Do you want to make that a combo with a drink?"

"Sure, a Coke. Thanks."

"Is that all, ma'am?"

"Yes."

"Okay, your total is [some embarrassingly small figure that explains the obesity epidemic]. Please drive up to your first window."

As I shut my window I catch Henry giving me the evil eye in the rearview mirror.

"I wanted a hamburger with cheese, not a cheeseburger."

"It's the same thing, Henry."

"It's going to taste weird."

"You're getting exactly what you want. Don't worry. A hamburger with cheese, okay?"

A small man in his McDonald's visor sticks his head out the small window. He is way farther out than he needs to be. I feel like he is going to jump into my car with me once I pull up next to him. He looks like he's around thirty years old, but I can't really tell because he's Filipino and Filipinos have that magic juice in them that keeps their faces flawless much longer than many other ethnicities.

The man takes my twenty-dollar bill and looks into the backseat. A smile stretches across his face. He's suddenly beaming.

"Oh! You have kids!" He leans out the window even farther, just to see them.

"Yeah, I do. I ordered two Happy Meals."

He's waving at them, like, really enthusiastically. "The cutest boys!"

"Thank you," Henry says, without a hint of irony.

He laughs.

I return a smile to the man, though mine is not meeting the levels of his enthusiasm at all. "That's sweet of you to say."

I catch Henry giving the McDonald's worker the side-eye; maybe it's because the man has not stopped staring at him or Aiden. The McDonald's guy is really, genuinely excited about these children; it's so earnest I have no idea how to interpret it.

"Hello!" he says to them. "Hello, boys!"

I turn and face Henry and Aiden, who look slightly confused, but they catch a glimpse of each other and begin to giggle, leaning on each other in this awkward moment.

Through a smile and gritted teeth I whisper to the boys, "Say hello, and we can go."

"Hi." They both half-muster sounds out of their mouth holes.

"Here!" The McDonald's worker passes me two extra Happy Meal toys.

Hmm, I guess this guy just really likes kids?

"Thanks. Wow, you really like kids!" I say, idiotically. I'm really terribly amateur at small talk. I make sure I'm smiling.

"I should like kids." He smiles back; I've fooled him. "I have four of them."

"Wow, four kids! You look so young!" Again, amateur move, men don't care about this compliment, but he nods and smiles more happily. "Four boys. They are thirteen, ten, seven, and five years old."

"That must be fun for you. Those are great ages!" I have no idea what I'm talking about. Now I'm ready to drive forward, get the kids their meals, bring them home, and stare at them for the next three hours before Aiden's mom arrives, relaxed and refreshed, to take her son home.

"They are in the Philippines"—he sighs, still smiling— "with my wife and mother. I haven't seen them in two years."

Uh, hold up . . . the Dolby surround sound in my hearing just cut out. Silence. The power dims in my brain, then flickers. I hear a piercing high-pitched frequency for a moment and then it vanishes.

I look back at this man and we now have had a weird pause and then I giggle awkwardly.

"What?" I break the silence with my stupid "what?"; my brain hasn't caught up to what he has just told me. No, seriously, what?

The man who hasn't seen his children in two years looks into the backseat again, and only now I see the wistfulness in the look. His eyes get misty, I think. I check my rearview and there are no cars lined up behind me. I'm there. His body language changes, he drapes his right arm across his chest and holds his left shoulder, hugging himself. The man is hugging himself. What have I done? I'm the fucking worst. This is what I fucking get for making small talk with a stranger, for fake smiling. I have to make this better. I could just give him these boys, right? He seems to like them. I rack my brain. I have to help this man. I toss out a line.

"You have Internet, though?"

He makes prayer hands to the sky. "Yes, we Skype two times a day. I came to Canada to work at McDonald's and send them money. It's much more money than I could have made there in a lifetime."

Jesus, Kelly. Shit. Shit. Shit. Keep smiling, fucking nod. Keep your fucking shit together for this man right now.

"I can grab the food for you."

He steps away from the window, packs our food in the bag and passes it to me, then drapes his arm back across his body and slightly rocks back and forth.

I smile like a crazy person, nodding.

"That's so great that you can Skype! Okay! Thanks. I hope I'll see you soon! I guess I will? I eat here a lot!"

"Great," he says, and waves good-bye to the boys.

I wave to him animatedly and he takes his hugging arm off his body and returns my insane wave.

I shut my window and, ventriloquist-style, through clenched teeth, say, "Wave 'bye to the man, Henry, wave 'bye to the man . . . Hen, Henry, wave 'bye to the man. *Aiden, you, too.*"

I drive by the window as slowly as possible . . . I see Henry and Aiden wave to the Filipino dad in the window, and the Filipino dad waves back to them and then I'm out of the McDonald's parking lot.

I turn on the radio, loud enough for the kids to be distracted and sing, and for me to quietly talk to myself about this event that just broke my brain apart at McDonald's.

I often talk to myself, TV monologue–style, when I drive.

These are the sorts of things a woman with small children, an anxiety disorder, and few local friends will do.

"Well," I whisper, "that was fucking brutal. I mean, I know this is a situation that happens all over the world. I've met nannies at the park that do this. But this guy had it so rough in the Philippines that he had to leave his kids to make money at a *McDonald's in Canada?* What the hell. What the bloody hell. I'm such an asshole; I refused to even get a job at McDonald's in high school. I'm a total cunt." I reach into the bag for a fry, but can't locate them through touch alone. Then I play critic to my own thinking. "But still? I know I'm just talking out of my ass. I'm in a place of privilege. I don't even have to work, and look at me. Driving around just to kill some time? I mean, this is probably a very positive thing for him, who the hell am I to judge? How great is it that he can come to Canada and get this job and send his family money until he can move them over here, right?"

"Right, Mom!" I look back and Henry's giving me the thumbs-up.

I guess I didn't realize how loud I was whispering.

"What's wrong?" Aiden asks, as the automatic garage door closes the winter out of the house. "Yeah, what's wrong?" Henry copies. They were privy to the same conversation I'd just heard. They're following the scent of cheese-burgers behind me, like little carnivore ducklings in Arctic clothing. They know.

"Nothing is wrong, really."

"Why hasn't that guy seen his kid in two years? That's sad. That's what made you really sad."

"Oh, you did hear that. No, I'm not sad. Maybe I'm a little sad because he forgot my fry order." I wasn't really upset about the fries. I mean, I love McDonald's fries but couldn't really blame the guy for forgetting them; that was a heavy conversation. He had other things on his mind.

I pull their boots off.

We walk up the stairs and to the dining room table. I am mindful of things now. How lucky I am. To be lucky enough to be alone with my kids for these years, when I absolutely could have been working overseas, or even here at home. Who am I to complain about playdates and my ineptitude in social graces?

I guess I just needed something to complain about. Because when I really think about it, I love playing Pirates and making inedible cookies with my kids to give to their dad to eat. I love driving them around, and I never really minded changing their diapers. What I didn't like was the repetition, but that's true of anything you do.

"So? Then are you sad about that guy forgetting your fries, and not his kids?"

"No, the kids made me sad. People should be able to hug their kids. A lot of people don't. But people are lucky to have jobs."

Henry pulls the paper back from his burger, performs a heavy inspection of its innards, takes a bite, and begins to talk with his mouth full.

"Are you ever going to go away to work, Mom? Away from us?"

"I hope not."

"Do you ever want to work?"

"Sure. Of course." I get up, pour some water for Henry and Aiden, and realize I forgot my Coke in the car.

"I don't ever want my mom to work for anyone but me." Aiden shakes his head and takes a bite of his burger.

I grab the paper towels, rip one off for Henry and one for Aiden. This is the repetition of my life.

"I don't want you to work, Mom, ever. I need you to keep doing this stuff."

"What stuff?"

Henry points at the kitchen, he points upstairs, he points at himself. "And Sal and Dad. That's your stuff. You're good at it, you can't stop."

"Okay." He looks at me, confused. I remember to smile. "I won't. I just have to run out to the garage for a second. I forgot my Coke in the car."

Henry and Aiden begin to talk to each other, swinging their legs, kicking the table.

I clench my mouth and run down the three stairs from the kitchen and turn to the door that leads to the garage. I prop it open and walk to the car, open the door, and pick up my Coke. In the dark cold of the garage, I sink into the driver's seat, knowing I can stay there for a moment.

Henry is right. I am good at my stuff. I give hamsters funerals. Whatever it is, whatever I'm doing, the kids happy. I'm lucky to be here, I'm lucky to be here. I am happy I know there are probably others like me, like Aiden's mom. Maybe she's alone sipping a McDonald's Coke right now, too? I am the village. I'm happy I don't have to send money across the world to my children I have to Skype twice a day.

I let the suction in my mouth go, relax, sip the Coke, wipe my eyes, and go back into the house.

Keeping Score

"Mom," she sighs, trying to roll her eyes but only succeeding in doing a strange-looking thing where her eyes dart back and forth. "I'm not going to school, ever again."

That is Beatrix Plum, my youngest child. A snappy octogenarian in a four-year-old's body. She says what she wants, when she wants to say it, and she doesn't think the consequences of speaking her mind are an issue.

She is a lot like Gram, and if my gram hadn't died *after* Beatrix was born, I'd believe she was Gram reincarnate.

At Gram's memorial Bea yelled, "She didn't even show up? She isn't even in a box for us to look at or anything?" Cremation was, apparently, "a boring choice."

I am tucking Beatrix into bed with her damp curling hair (she hates the blow-dryer) and freshly minty baby teeth. Her top two front ones have indents in them from the pacifier she would not let go of until she was three. Bea's face is so cute I want to eat it. I know, I know, I know you're thinking, *So what?* and *God, this is really boring already, a mom who thinks her kid is cute. What a fucking revelation.* I am her mother; of course I think she's adorable. I am absolutely, boom-box-over-my-head in love with my children. I just have to write that down. When I'm dead and gone, in my urn (I also want to be cremated. Sorry, Bea!), I will be satisfied knowing that I really put in the effort to explain how chubby my kids' cheeks were and how soft their eyes were and how much I wanted to scoop their whole sweet, soft faces out like a cantaloupe and eat them every single day.

"Bea, you're going to school tomorrow unless I eat you first. Let's read a book. Isn't this fun?" *Isn't this fun?* is my go-to when things aren't really fun in parenting. A diversion tactic, like when my mom used to tell me that the brown spots on bananas were sugar.

I kiss her cheek, pressing my lips as far into that squish as I can and stopping right before I know I would be hurting her.

"I am not going to school. I don't like it there." The tone

of her voice sets off an alarm; I feel the mom panic creeping into my body.

I try to stop the thoughts that pop up. What is happening to my child when she isn't with me? This is preschool, she gets to sing songs, paint with her hands, have books read to her, and play with toys she doesn't own. I tilt my head like a dog listening for more clues.

"Why don't you like school?"

She shuts her eyes. "It's stupid."

I press, now I need all the answers. "Anything else?"

"Nope!" She pops the *p* at the end of her sentence and smiles. I can leave this for now; I don't need to get worked up before I go to bed.

"Let's read."

"Okay, okay." She attempts the eye roll again, eyes darting weirdly around in their sockets, and drops her arms on top of her floral bedspread. I hold up a Halloween-themed book with a very cutesy stylized skeleton on it. Skeletons with personalities have always bothered me. I mean, at least with anthropomorphism, animals have brains. Skeletons are just bones. You can't make a meal out of an empty fridge. Leave skeletons out of it.

"I think your skeleton would be this cute," I lovingly say to her.

"My skeleton? What skeleton?" she asks earnestly. "I don't have one."

I look deep into her eyes. Watching your child discover something for the first time is incredible. Like the first time they realize that poop and pee are made of food and drinks.

KELLY OXFORD

They are part disgusted, part amazed, and think it's completely hilarious.

One afternoon Bea and I were watching TV when a commercial for a charity for disabled veterans came on. Images of amputees faded into each other.

"How long does it take for her legs to grow back?" Bea asked. "Like, a year or something?" Or the time I turned on a documentary about Hawaii. *"Volcanoes are real things?!"*

Those are the moments parents live for, the moments that give us the energy to keep going.

"Yes, you do have a skeleton, Bea."

"No."

"Bea, you have a skeleton of bones inside of you. There is a skeleton inside of me, and everyone. There *is* a skeleton inside of you!"

"THERE IS A SKELETON IN ME?" She lies motionless on her pillow with her stuffed panda by her head. With her delicious chubby fingers she fiddles with the panda's foot, then her hand moves to her elbow and she investigates the bones. She's registering what I'm saying as fast as her eyes are filling with tears. Her mouth pulls down at the corners, her eyes squeeze shut so hard they eat her eyelashes as a heavy tear pops from the side of her eye and rolls down the side of her face. She whispers, but forcefully whispers, *"Get it out. Get the skeleton out."*

"I can't, Bea! You need it! It's like the Popsicle stick that the Popsicle sticks to! Your body is meat, it needs your skeleton to hold it up, uhh, like a coat on a coat hanger."

"Mom, you're annoying me so much I'm gonna O. J. Simpson you."

THE NEXT DAY, AFTER dropping Bea off at preschool in the afternoon, I ask James if we can quickly pop in to Chipotle. "How did I live without Chipotle in Calgary?"

"You went to McDonald's a lot."

"Well, I don't like the McDonald's here quite as much. The meat, lettuce, and cheese are not the same as at home. Everyone thinks I'm crazy for saying that, but they're the crazy ones. Do they think Mexican McDonald's source from the same companies for the produce and meat? Do they think England does?"

"Kelly, they probably don't think about it at all." James is still circling the parking lot, looking for a spot. I can sense his annoyance.

"Someone here told me that McDonald's doesn't use real eggs and I was like, I *saw* the eggs being cracked in Canada. McDonald's is definitely better in Canada, those lettuce farmers up there are on point."

Being in America was strange, not just because the McDonald's situation was sadder. Overall, the negatives of living in a metropolis of 3.9 million over a city of 1 million were very apparent to me all the time. I could sense my stress levels were much, much higher in the US.

"Have I been more high-strung since we moved here?" I ask James.

"Yes."

"Well, you weren't supposed to say yes like that. God, now I'm even more stressed." I think about Beatrix's spiral the night before. How her not liking preschool instantly made me worry. How her worries about having a skeleton made her cry. Some dogs are bred to be retrievers, and I feel like I was bred to try to solve everyone's problem with the most efficiency possible. Here, in Los Angeles, there are almost four times more people whose energy I had to deflect than there were in Calgary. It's exhausting. And I can see that it is exhausting James and the kids, too. It leaves me feeling very guilty, like I'm responsible for their new reality of living in a city like Los Angeles. Every incessant honk fest or whiff of street urine triggers thoughts of *Oh, this is my fault"* Or *This wouldn't happen at home. Man, it was so much nicer at home, right? I'm putting my poor family through all of this!*

We don't need to be here. James would pack it in tomorrow. But I want it to work for us. I want us to live here, mostly for the weather.

"Oh, there's a spot. Right in front of Chipotle!" I clap my hands, like I've just witnessed a teenage girl balk at men's expectations.

"You're clapping?"

"It's Chipotle, an American institution. Who wouldn't clap? An idiot. That's who. Isn't this fun?!"

We walk up the dirty wheelchair ramp, through the heavy glass door, and immediately see and hear a commotion that isn't a regular afternoon Chipotle commotion. Through the restaurant and out the back window I see an ambulance, lights flashing.

I ask James if he can see anything. He's only six foot two, but at five foot six and a half, I insist on treating him like my personal periscope. We cross the floor, heading toward the end of the order line.

"Oh shit."

I'm not sure how we missed him, perhaps it was the blinding burrito desire, but there, on the floor, is a man. He's lying on his side with two paramedics kneeling beside him. The older paramedic has his fingers on the man's neck, checking his pulse. The paramedic shakes his head and rolls the man over.

"Oh my God," I whisper as the younger medic begins to give the man chest compressions. I gasp and cover my mouth.

"James, is he dying in Chipotle?!"

Two things flash through my mind: 1.) I have never seen a human dying. 2.) I have never seen a human die.

I watch in horror as the paramedics pump his gray-haired chest between the sides of his Tommy Bahama button-up.

From behind us, a finger taps James on the shoulder. James and I both turn and look. Standing there are an annoyed-looking blond guy and a thin brunette, maybe forty-five years old. I try to figure out if they've recognized us, if I know them, but I don't recognize them at all.

"Isn't this horrible?" I prepare to tell them we missed what had happened to Tommy Bahama, when the man motions past us with his hands. Motioning us to move along.

"The line is moving," he says, eyebrows up, encouraging us to move forward toward burritos.

KELLY OXFORD

James and I turn around and see there is a space of at least seven people between us and the people ahead of us.

"Oh, right." James grabs my sleeve and steps up to the man ahead of us in line. When we stop, I lean into him and look back to the man getting chest compressions.

"The line is still moving? People are ordering Chipotle while Tommy Bahama is dying?"

"People are still ordering burritos." He lets my arm go and takes in the scene. "We're all in a line, walking around a dying man, to order burritos. This is immeasurably fucked up." A third paramedic enters Chipotle wheeling in a stretcher, and stops beside the other two, who are still giving chest compressions. They lift the man onto the stretcher as we take a few steps forward in the line.

"This is the most fucked-up thing I've ever seen," he whispers.

"And we're part of it! This is *not* fun."

The medic who brought in the stretcher lifts up a defibrillator. I can't stop staring at the dying man as we reach the counter.

The young Chipotle woman says, "Hello!"

My mouth opens and out comes, "Noooo. Wait. Stop. This is so wrong. That man is dying."

James ignores the woman, he's floored. "Is this is a joke? This would never happen in Canada."

"James, of course it wouldn't happen in Canada, no one wears Tommy Bahama in the winter."

I attempt to defuse this new situation, as I have been

attempting to defuse what feels like Every. Single. Thing. Since we moved here. We're almost forty and experiencing new things like this, things we would never see in Canada, every day. And here's the truth—we have moved here; let's really immerse ourselves in this stuff, you know? We're in Los Angeles now, we have to expect that things won't be the same and not judge this place so harshly. This is not Canada. It's just different. McDonald's doesn't crack their eggs, and I have to accept it.

"James, this is a big city and these things happen. Look, those paramedics are doing a great job. We're the weirdos here, look around. Everyone wants to order Chipotle but us!" We really were the only people who appeared to have moral issues with ordering a burrito bowl while a man's heart was being shocked beside us. Maybe it was us? Maybe there really wasn't anything wrong with what was happening.

James is still looking at the man. "Maybe instead of looking at the man being defibrillated, we should be looking at the Chipotle menu, right?"

I point to the menu but my shaking finger is proof that I don't even believe a thing I am saying. James takes my hand. "I've lost my appetite. Let's go to the grocery store and buy some stuff for dinner." I turn to the obviously hungry couple behind us. "Go ahead." We walk toward the back door of Chipotle and look over our shoulders at the paramedics wheeling Tommy Bahama out the front door.

"This is such an LA thing," James subtly chastises.

"It's not an LA thing." I try to sound as though I have the conviction of a Supreme Court justice, preferably Ruth Bader Ginsburg, but basically any one of them but Clarence Thomas. "This could happen in any big city."

And, as if on cue, peeking into the Chipotle, holding the door with one hand and his bike with the other, is Ed Begley Jr., wearing a bike helmet. LA 1, Kelly Oxford 0.

"MOM, I'M NOT GOING to school today," Bea says at the breakfast table the day after the Chipotle episode, folding her arms across her chest, her curly hair wild from air-drying in her sleep.

"And I'm not eating breakfast. My teeth are weak." She nods and pinches her eyes closed for effect.

James laughs. "Your teeth are fine. I'm forty and I have never had a cavity, you have the enamel DNA of a superhero. Eat your breakfast."

Salinger walks in, opens a cupboard, grabs a bowl and the cereal, and helps herself to breakfast. Her teeth are not weak.

"I had Cheesecake Factory ranch sauce for the first time last night. It was so good."

"Guess what, Sal? I'm not going to school today," Bea half yells into the table.

Sal gives Bea the side-eye. "Interesting."

"Oh, yes, you are," James says, old-school dad in full force.

"Oh my God, Bea!" Henry is nine years old and stuffing his face full of waffles. I casually walk by and slice some bananas onto his plate of carbohydrates. If I ask, he'll say no. If I just add them without asking, he will eat them. I think. As long as "there isn't a lot of brown in the centers," which could also be a basic motto for life.

Henry sighs, "Bea, you're in *preschool*!" Henry is our only son and middle child, and if he is thinking it, you hear about it. He's a superb storyteller, joke teller, an excellent mentor for many of my friends' younger children. Impressed with Henry's ability to make conversation and point out the obvious in things, a senior editor at *GQ*, only half kidding, told me that they have an internship waiting for Henry when he's done with school. Henry's response, "Oh, yeah. Great! No, wait, I am interning at Danny's studio and producing that Ninja Roommate show with Anne Hathaway. Too bad. I guess maybe if that doesn't work out?" Henry is part Ferris Bueller, part Max Fischer.

Now he moans, "I would *kill* to be in preschool! You don't have to do anything! You draw and sing! Bea! It's *awesome*. Stop it. I have to do sooooo much work."

"What? You're in the fourth grade, Henry. Shut up." In chimes Salinger, the oldest Cheesecake Factory connoisseur.

Sal eats her cereal. "Mom, have you ever tried the ranch sauce at The Cheesecake Factory? I don't know what they do to it. It's so, so good." I walk over to the fridge and pull the heavy stainless-steel door open. "Sal, I think if you make more than one reference to Cheesecake Factory ranch sauce before eight a.m., you're officially American." I pause, looking over the options for Bea. "Bea, you have to eat something for breakfast. What about an egg, that won't hurt your teeth."

"Ewwwwww."

"What if you just have a banana?"

"I don't. Want. Anything."

"Bea, you have to eat something. Hey, hey, hey!" I catch Henry stepping on the garbage bin opener, about to slide his sliced banana into the bin.

"Eat that, Henry!"

"Gross." He pulls the plate back and fakes retching onto it.

"You know what happens to kids who don't eat fruit and vegetables? They get cancer." I mean, eventually. Probably. Not eating fruit or vegetables certainly doesn't help the body.

"I like strawberries."

"We're out."

"Well, I'll eat those."

"Me too!" Bea shouts, her head on the table.

"Fine, when you're at school, Dad and I will stop at the grocery store and get you some."

"Make sure they're grown local!" Henry dumps his food into the bin, throws his Clippers hat on, and walks out of the kitchen.

I've felt responsible for the impression the city of Los Angeles is making on my husband and kids since the moment we moved here. Like every new metropolitan difficulty we now live with (traffic, crime, entitled strangers) is some sort of proof we shouldn't be here, despite all the positive (friends, great weather) that comes of being here, the negative of the city seems to outweigh it all. James freaks out and says, "We're going home," at least three times a week. And I have to admit, I get it. I don't like people pushing me in the drugstore. I don't like when the driver ahead of me stops in the middle of the street to get something out of their trunk. This is all very exhausting for me. I don't necessarily think it's fair, but I also feel that James's inability to get a job here in the States can't really be helped when he doesn't yet have a green card. I'm trying to keep him happy in traffic, get my kids to school, and make sure they're happy and also work and support everyone. I mean, they were very excited to move here; in fact, it was James's idea, but when it comes down to it, this was my dream. Not theirs.

I sit in the car, while James is in the grocery store getting local strawberries. I need to defuse. Nobody likes to feel like everything is working against them, but today I just feel like the city is against me. I mean, Sal has her ranch dressing now, so that's a blessing, but otherwise it hasn't all been Cheesecake Factory bliss. I understand why I defend LA and try to make James feel as though things are status quo, it's because I want everyone to be happy. I want to accept the chaos as our new life, but now I'm overwhelmed, and it feels like a battle at every turn.

I'm thinking about all of this as I look out the window of the car. I'm glazed over, my eyes unfocused, until something swift and large dashes in front of the windshield. A large man in an oversize (even on him) red T-shirt and open beige jacket is running, well, limping and sort of hopping away from the grocery store, holding his stomach strangely. He's headed toward me. The shutting electronic door of the grocery store suddenly opens again and it's a security guard, who's chasing after the big guy in the red shirt. The door opens again and it's James casually walking out of the store, also catching the commotion.

"Oh, shit. What is happening?"

Like I would in a nightmare, I watch James and the security guard run toward the man in the red shirt.

The limping large guy turns back toward the grocery store; he sees that the security guard and James are chasing him. Immediately, he releases his grasp on the front of his shirt and, I can't tell exactly what it is, but a pile of crap falls from his belly onto the parking lot. Limping guy is a shoplifter. The large man turns back toward me, away from the security guard and James, and immediately and directly crashes his body into a parked car. Upon impact, two large bottles of liquor fall from his shirt and smash onto the parking lot pavement, then the man slides down the car onto the pavement on top of the puddles of liquor and glass.

Like walking away from an explosion, James watches the security guard tackle the man and walks right past them to me. He opens the door.

"Did you see that? That guy had at least a dozen steaks and, like, two bottles of vodka up his shirt and got tackled." I nod. "Pretty fun, right?" LA 2, Kelly Oxford 0.

"I DON'T WANT TO go to school." Bea is in her booster seat, pouting. She refused to eat breakfast, even the strawberries we bought yesterday. Bea and I have been in the car for twenty minutes already, driving Henry to his school and Sal to hers. Having kids not so close in age made a lot of things easier on me: one kid in diapers at a time, one in school while the other was at home, two in school while the third was at home. But a few things were more difficult, and mostly, now, the school situation. There is a lot of driving to be done in the very early hours in the morning with three children who are just age-gapped enough to always be attending different schools. Different schools mean different events to attend, different parents to be friends with. It is like living in three different worlds at the same time. Most days I barely have it in me to care about one of these worlds; it sucks that there are three. If there were a reasonable opportunity to have all of my kids in the same school I would have grabbed it a long time ago, but I'm not willing, nor wealthy enough, to pay $40K per child for an elementary education in a private school that's pre-K through 12. By the end of it, that's a little more than $1.5 million I'd spend on grade school, not to mention the money the school would hound us for in donations. For $1.5 million, my kids had better graduate from school running Fortune 500 companies. I grew up not being able to have jeans that cost $40. Fuck that. And so I spend hours driving them to and from three different public schools, every day, saying, "Fuck that. Fuuuuuuuck that. Fuck that."

"Bea, you're going to have fun at school! There will be stories and art. Will you make me some art?"

"No. I am not going to have fun at school. It's boring,"

she squawks. She sits quietly for a moment and then shouts, "*Oh, man!* My brain keeps saying a bad word."

Great. "What word, Bea?"

"Frickin'. It's saying frickin'. Oh great, now it's saying frickin' *and* shit!"

"Well, you keep those words in your head today, okay?" I turn on the radio.

"Ohh, it's that Nicki Massage song. Turn it up."

Bea and I walk into her Montessori preschool class. She is dragging her feet and is now very quiet. I sign her in and she holds my leg, rubbing her cheek into my outer thigh. If you've ever looked at an abandoned puppy and almost cried about how perfect it is, that's the same feeling a mother gets when her child is genuinely this affectionate and needy. Yes, I just compared my child to a dog. It happens. Some people aren't kid people and you have to walk them through this stuff.

"I don't want to be here," she whispers sadly, eyes welling with tears. I suddenly feel like grabbing her and running from that beautiful preschool like it's a sex slave encampment. It's irrational and exactly what I'm expecting from myself when I'm already this stressed and I can't solve a problem immediately and efficiently—all I want to do is run. She's really acting like I'm leaving her in some horrible child labor camp, clinging to me, whispering, "Don't leave me here." I look around at the women who run the school and wonder if they are capable of being monsters. Because what if that were the case and Bea was pleading to stay with me because she had a monster for a teacher, someone who neglected or abused the kids at every opportunity? Now I'm sick to my stomach. I just go there, I can't help myself. My mind is a constantly burning imagination brushfire of worry, and torture and abuse are like kindling. Could the teachers be yelling? Smacking their hands? Ignoring these wonderful little toddler assholes? I bend down to Bea, and very gravely, we look at each other.

I hug her and, feeling the wispy tendrils of her hair on my lips, I whisper into her ear, "Okay, so, why don't you want to be here?" I wait for it, eying the Polish schoolmarm, Mrs. Chelbek, on the other side of the rug, ready for the worst. Ready to throw down an ultimate beating if the moment calls for it.

"I mean, Bea, I certainly haven't seen your teacher do anything wrong, myself. She is very well organized, she has a fun class, and is, at worst, slightly cold, but she's Eastern European, so 'slightly cold' is actually really pretty warm." She's ignoring me. I'm poised and ready to tell Bea that if there has been something terrible, therapy will help whatever it is that's been happening in that classroom, and I'm always there for her. That's when Bea leans back, looks me in the eye as she points to a chair that says BEA, and slowly Eeyore-moans, "*I hate having to sit in the same chair every day*. I don't want to be here because I have to sit in the same chair."

Wait. "That's it?" I ask.

"Yes!"

Oh, no. She's me.

I kiss her forehead and stand up, shaking Bea off my

leg. I lock eyes with Mrs. Chelbek. "See you at two forty-five." I turn to Bea. "It will go by quickly. Try to enjoy yourself. I mean, if you can't enjoy yourself in preschool, you're screwed."

She's screwed.

My phone rings while I'm waiting in traffic; it's Bea's school. Really? I put the phone on speaker.

"Hello?"

"Hi, this is Mrs. Chelbek. Beatrix says she really needs to talk to you and then she will go back to her work. Since you left, she has been causing a bit of a fuss about wanting to go home, but she calmed down when I told her she could call you. I'm putting her on the phone."

"Okay."

Bea's voice sounds sick, tired. "Mooooom?"

"Yeah? Bea, I just left you. What's up?"

She whispers, "I tricked my teacher into letting me call you. Come get me." I pull over on the side of a tree-lined street and place my phone, on speaker, on the armrest.

"I can't, Bea. You have to stay at your school while I go to work for a bit and then in no time I'll come pick you up. Just pretend the BEA chair is some sort of game. It will be fun!!"

"Mom, you have to pick me up now."

"Bea, every kid goes to school. There is nothing wrong with your school. It's lovely. You will get over this, okay? I promise. You've only been there for a few minutes."

"A few minutes? I come here every day for the whole day!" She then whispers, "Some kids here have diapers!"

"Bea, it's October, you've only been in school for a few months. It will get better, okay?"

"But it's more fun at home with you."

"Everyone goes to school."

"But, Mom, they don't love me here."

I feel that thump. That deep-down parental thump, the one that aches like guilt. "What?"

"There are so many kids here. In Miss Sudeep's class in Canada everyone knew everyone. No one here knows me or loves me and that's scary. Miss Sudeep loved me."

She was right. Her LA preschool was nothing like the one in Calgary. I check over my left shoulder for traffic and my phone flies off the middle armrest as I pull a wide U-turn across four lanes. I lean toward my phone on the ground on the passenger side. "I'm coming to get you, tell your teacher."

Mrs. Chelbek seems annoyed with the disruption Bea and I have caused her classroom full of kids sitting at labeled chairs, counting beads from one bowl to another. I don't blame her. I suddenly see the monotony in all of these Montessori "exercises." Without the obvious love, and in such big numbers, counting beads and sewing squares made it look like the kids were in a sweatshop training camp. We were totally breaking their imaginative minds down into believing that taskwork is life. . . . I mean, that does have its place if you want a life knitting sweaters or making jewelry for Etsy or something. But not if you're four and want to feel connected to someone or something. I was so troubled with the notion that Bea even understood what it felt like to be that lonely and uncared for. I was paying these people good money to care for her all day while I worked, not to make her feel lonely.

"I think she'll be fine and you should try leaving her here today," Chelbek says to me, while I stand with her near the door of the school. We are facing away from Bea, but I take a peek back at her. She is giving us the stare down from her BEA chair. When she sees me looking, she grits her teeth and says, "I'm not allowed to get up."

Chelbek turns and catches this transpiring and continues, "Sometimes this happens to kids who are just being introduced to Montessori."

I feel my defenses coming up. "She had no problem with Montessori in Canada. I mean, I did. I hated it. I wouldn't do the fake naptime or anything. I made them call my dad to pick me up on the first day."

"Well, if Bea wants to attend our school, we don't want to promote this sort of event. I'm not sure how you do Montessori *in Canada,* but here, we drop the children off without a spectacle."

"*In Canada,* it's the same thing. She also takes ballet and other classes and is fine. She just has a problem with this class, your class in particular."

Upon hearing this, Chelbek's neck jerks her head into a tilt and I see her slim tongue slightly wet her pinched lips. Gross.

"This class? There isn't a problem with this class. Maybe she is just taking after her mother? Like you said, you left your class."

That's it, I make the decision to go full cuckoo. "Well, you know what? She told me on the phone that you don't love her."

Her eyebrows furrow. "What?"

I step back, away from her; I feel like Adam Sandler in a loud monologue. "Yeah, she feels lonely, over there with sixty kids. Two of them are pulling out their own hair at the table! I think they're scared!"

"Excuse me; please keep your voice down. You are being totally inappropriate. I have never had a problem with any of my students. Maybe it's your child that isn't a fit for us."

"My child? Do you even know her name without looking at that chair?"

She starts to turn her glare to the chair; I put my hand out.

"Don't look at the chair!!" I gasp. "And look, that kid over there is crying!" A little blond girl colors bright pink as she weeps in her GRACE chair.

"She always cries, you don't know." Chelbek says this with the coldness of an Arctic spy.

"Lady! That isn't cool!"

"I don't mean to be rude, but are you mentally ill?" she asks.

"Oh, probably."

I walk over to Bea, in her little BEA chair, and she looks up at me. "Are you done? I've been faking counting this whole time. Can we go now?"

I nod, on a mission to get her as fast as I can out of this place where she counts beads in a loveless room.

"Yep." She hops up, skips to her cubby, grabs her lunch

bag, and continues to skip to the doorway. Standing near Chelbek, Bea smiles into her cold face. I take the BEA off the back of the chair, and walk to Bea. I grab her hand and stop at Chelbek, speaking quietly and closely, so Bea can't hear.

"Sorry I went berserk. I have issues. I'm canceling my checks. Sorry your school wasn't a fit for us. I'm sure you are a very lovely lady deep down."

I LOOK FOR TRAFFIC and open the car door for Bea, at the metered parking on the street outside of the coffee shop. I still haven't made it home since I left on this morning's round of dropping the kids off. I balance the tray of two coffees and apple juice on the roof as she climbs in. We all need drinks to enjoy while I explain to James that Bea is a preschool dropout and will not be going to school for the rest of the year because I lost my mind. I felt all of my kid issues resurface and blow up in Bea's class. I knew all of the other preschools were full. That should have been the first sign that Chelbek's school was terrible: they let us in.

"Are you sad at all?" I ask Bea, as I stand back on the sidewalk, watching her do up her seatbelt, which she insists on doing herself. "You're never going to see any of those kids again. I mean, I don't have any of their numbers or anything."

"No. We weren't even really allowed to talk to each other in there. Hold on, I'm thirsty." Bea stops trying to buckle her seat belt and reaches her hand toward me; I open the apple juice container and put it in her hand. She takes a sip from the glass opening, sucking her mouth into the round container. When she snaps it off her face, I can see a tiny apple juice mustache on her upper lip. She makes a face, closing her eyes. "Chelbek was a weird young lady. She wasn't a good fit."

"Bea, she wasn't young. She was older than me."

"She was not older than you. People older than you have gray hair. Her hair isn't gray, it's brown," she tells me, like I'm the biggest idiot in the entire world. But I have the upper hand because I'm not a child. I know things, a great many things she has not learned, and we are about to have a "moment."

"Bea, she is old. She colors her hair brown, it's really gray. She colors it at a salon like Auntie Lauren's salon. She's probably the same age as your grammy. Please don't tell Grammy I called her old."

Bea licks the apple juice from the tiny downy hairs on her upper lip, her eyebrows furrowed. She's processing this information. Realizing that people color their hair, but none of the older people in her life do.

"Mrs. Chelbek colors her gray hair brown so people don't know she's an old lady?"

I nod. "Yes, a lot of people do that. Now, give me that apple juice and get into your seat."

"Weird."

Bea notices a man and his bulldog that are about to pass us—"Awwwwww"—distracted from the seat belt again. *She should be sorting beads,* I think. . . . *Shut up,* I think. . . . The man with the bulldog stops. "He's friendly, you can call him. His name is Harold." The man smiles wide at Bea, like he's introducing his son to her.

"Awww, Harold, come here, boy. Oh, man, he is so slobbery, Mom!" The man chuckles to himself, admiring his dog. "Harold, you want to go see the little girl?" he asks the white bulldog.

The "my kid meets your kid" thing with dog owners really creeps me out. I'm suddenly feeling very on edge again, very aware of all of my neuroses and judgment and wonder how all of my reactionary stuff is being passed along to my kid. I hated day care for the same reason Bea hated that school. Was this stuff learned or were we all predisposed genetically? Was Bea going to be loud and rude like my gram and me because we were loud and maybe viewed as rude; is it in our DNA? Maybe she will take after James.

"Aww," the man says, watching his animal slobber all over my kid's hands, "Harold, you like her, don't you, boy?"

He smiles again, at Bea. "Harold likes you. What's your name?"

Bea turns, and motions for me to bend down to her. "Tell him I'm not answering him because he's wearing a stupid Yankees cap."

Yep. Nature not nurture.

A HELICOPTER OVERHEAD, I walk up the hot asphalt parking lot with Bea, carrying James's coffee, passing other hot, tired people and wondering how I would explain her presence to him.

"Dad's gonna be so happy I don't go to school anymore!"

Bea smiles as I squeeze her hand. "Oh, he's going to be really surprised!" I'm hoping he keeps his worries about her dropping out to himself until she's out of earshot.

"Are we going to be at the grocery store for long? I hate getting groceries. I do like the coconut balls, though."

I don't want her to be scarred or anything, it's not like she needs another year of preschool anyhow. I also don't want her to think she can dictate how long we spend grocery shopping. Life isn't all coconut balls. I figure I will have to play this one with caution.

"Hey!" A homeless man appears on the sidewalk beside Bea, he's bent over, looking at her. *"Your mom did this to me!!"*

He shows her his arms, they are covered in fresh blood. Blood is dripping all over the ground, it's on his T-shirt. Neither we, nor the man, stop walking and soon we are feet away from each other. I am in shock. Bea's mouth hangs open.

"I didn't do that to him!" I yell. *"I did not do that to him!"*

I scan Bea for blood.

"Who the heck was that?" Bea asks, as we watch two police cruisers, lights on, enter the parking lot. I point them in the direction at the man who has accused me of stabbing him in the arms.

It then occurs to me that the helicopter was following him. Three more police cars enter the lot.

"What is happening?" Bea asks.

"That man with the blood needs help. He is very confused."

"Because you stabbed him."

"I didn't. You were with me."

"Why would he say that?"

"He's confused."

He was confused. He wasn't scary, or threatening, just confused. And now this huge police presence was confusing me. There were six cars, and two officers were pointing guns at the man with the bloody arms. He just stood in front of the grocery store, unarmed, bleeding and talking to himself. I wished he would just lie down and get cuffed. Even though he had falsely accused me of a stabbing I did not commit, I didn't want him to get shot, especially while my kid who just dropped out of preschool was watching. LA 3, Kelly Oxford 0.

"Let's go see Dad."

"Dad, Dad!" Bea runs breathlessly over to James in the frozen foods aisle. I'm right behind her, so he doesn't lose his mind.

"Bea! You aren't in school!?"

She holds on to his pant leg and sways. "I can't go there, no one cares about me and some kids wear diapers."

"Oh?" James's eyebrows, naturally thinner than mine, go up as he looks over to me. I nod to confirm what Bea is saying.

"And Mom *stabbed a man*." Half the people in Trader Joe's look my way.

"I didn't stab him!" I reach into the basket and pull out a treat. "You want a coconut ball?"

• • •

"SHE DIDN'T EVEN SEEM to be really freaked out by the whole thing," I whisper across the kitchen to James, as we unpack groceries together.

"Because you didn't seem fazed by it. You handled it well."

"Thanks."

"I can't believe I missed that," James says. "I would have punched that bleeding-arm guy in the face."

"No, you wouldn't have. You're Canadian."

"We punch the most because we don't carry guns. So Bea isn't going back to that school?'

"No, she made her case very clear. I felt the same way when I was a kid once and it was terrible. I promised I would never do the same to my kids."

Bea scoops the last of the coconut balls into her mouth. "Can I have another?"

"No, you can't, what we can do is find you a new school."

Bea nods thoughtfully. "Not in Canada, though."

"No?"

"No." She smiles. "This place is way too fun."

There Is a Man Who Powders His Balls

"Sometimes the dog just hops up on his back when we're having sex and goes for a ride," Lila's mom says as she shakes a spoon back and forth above my plate, depositing a pile of stringy, creamy mac and cheese onto it. Her hand raises the now empty greasy spoon and points it directly at me. "That's the sort of thing that keeps marriages together."

"Oh." I nod, wondering if my eyebrows are furrowed enough.

"Right. Yes. Totally makes sense!"

I break eye contact and gaze across the room. My eyes land on Lila's dad. He sits peacefully in his reading chair, stroking the family's small toy poodle sitting on his lap. I look at them, in their innocent repose, then turn back to my food, as I've begun to desperately fight my brain to prevent it visualizing the poodle surfing Lila's dad's hairy back, which I know is very hairy, because he wears thin white T-shirts. But there I am, dipping my fork into the mac and cheese, visions of the poodle balancing on his back as he grunts and sweats, heaving back and forth.

I'm slightly thankful that Lila is in the bathroom and has missed this entire transaction, as I'm sure she would have stopped her mother from sharing these details of monogamy with me. She's been in there so long, she is surely taking a dump.

"You know?" Lila's mom laughs like *she's* the seventeen-year-old at the table, tucking a lock of her thick, gray, spiraled hair behind her ear. "Sometimes you just let a dog go for a ride!"

I nod and dig into the glistening macaroni. "Oh, yeah!" I shift and glance back at the poodle. "I get it!"

Um, hello . . . I totally don't get it, and also, I have a few questions:

1. Has the poodle ever fallen off? If yes, did you stop, did she bounce off the floor a little because of that puffy poodle fur, or did you just keep boning, realizing it later when you watched your sex tape? I assume any-

one allowing dogs in on monogamous lovemaking also
records it.

2.   Does the poodle walk around while she's up there
on his back? Giving Dad a little massage with those
teeny little feet? Because that sounds relaxing but also
like some sort of animal sexual enslavement.

3.   Does the entire family consider this act to be poodle
agility training? Assuming the entire family knows about
this. Which surely they do, considering how freely Lila's
mom is sharing with me.

Unfortunately, I don't get the chance to ask any of these questions, because I can hear my friend Lila's footsteps creaking and squeaking on the old hardwood in her bathroom, after her laborious dump. I don't ask these questions I would like answers to because I'm just that good a friend.

Lila's mom must sense this special sharing moment is over, now that Lila has returned from working her bodily functions. I am quite happy I was told the information about the back-riding sex dog, and I wish more people communicated like Lila's mother.

My husband does not communicate like Lila's mother. He forgets to get right to the good stuff. He makes me work for the conversation. I need to ask the right questions, carefully following his twisted path of reasoning, or I'm left utterly confused.

"I understand what it's like to be a woman," James says on his second cup of sake. I'm finishing up my fourth, and after that sentence I'm on to the fifth. It's date night on

Ventura Boulevard in Studio City, which is basically a designated sushi district, so we're having sushi, because we're not that original. We sit across from each other in the darkness of Kazu Sushi, being served the chef's choice. It's heaven. A fresh, fixed menu like this is probably the closest I'll ever come to being some sort of revered, fat Japanese emperor who has people to adorn his rooms with hand-lettered poetry, and this is really unfortunate, because I think that lifestyle and aesthetic would be amazing. In images of Japanese nobles they are always smiling because of the great food, those cute, unrestrictive wrestling diapers, and their perfect topknots.

"Please, don't ever say you know what it feels like to be a woman," I tell him, eyeballing the last of my fifth sake and now contemplating a sixth. "You have no fucking clue."

"Kelly?" James leans in, deadly serious. "I'm fairly worldly. In fact, I'd say I'm a renaissance man."

I immediately pour the sixth and get sloppy. "Whatever, you saw babies come out of my vagina and didn't freak out, you like Pinterest, and you *have* bought me tampons, Monistat, and pregnancy tests."

"See?" He shrugs. "Renaissance."

"It's 2016; we now call that woke."

(Props: My husband actually buys me a lot of pregnancy tests because I have polycystic ovary syndrome, which is a real hoot. It makes you miss periods and have prolonged periods and gives you three-month pregnancy bloat, constantly!)

"But none of that means you know what it's like to be

a woman. Don't ever repeat that, to anyone. Especially my staunch feminist friends. I mean, even my regular feminist friends, which are basically all of my friends, okay? I like them, I need them, and I don't want to lose them. Saying that will make them all hate me for being married to you."

"Kelly, I'm alone in West Hollywood all the time. Gay men are everywhere. My gym is a gay gym. I know what it's like to be leered at by men. I get it."

"Oh my God, that's your entire argument? You know what it's like to be a woman because you've also had men look at you? Ha!" I take and drink that sixth cup of sake, and as I do, I process what he has just told me and as usual immediately come up with a long series of questions.

"Wait. So, at this gym, you're feeling what? One. Sexually vulnerable? Two. Pursued? Three. Sexy as hell?" I slide my teeth over a boiled edamame shell, popping the beans into my mouth.

"Yes! Basically all of those." I can sense he feels relief in my empathy.

I toss my shell into the shell plate. "Wait. Don't men feel that way when women hit on them?"

"I've never had a woman hit on me."

"You're such an idiot. Look, I know this isn't a cool thing to say on date night . . ." Oh, and by the way, for those of you who aren't parents, referring to a night out with your significant other as "date night" feels like equal parts relief from the kids and acceptance that your life is over.

"You do know that straight guys thinking they're being hit on by gay guys is a cliché? Everyone laughs at straight guys who believe this, like *hahaha, look at how stupid straight guys are.* You aren't being hit on. Trust me."

"Are you seriously trying to diminish my experience? You have no idea. You aren't there."

The waiter arrives with our salmon: tiny pieces of fish, beautifully piggybacking on tinier piles of rice.

"I'm giving it to you straight." I laugh at my own pun, but forge on, for the good of mankind. I repeat, "You aren't being hit on."

"Well, I am, and thanks a lot for the support," James argues, with nothing to back his claim. "I bet all the straight men who claim gay men hit on them are right. We understand men because we are men. We're all about sex."

"I can assure you that in the gay community where this is discussed, straight men are notorious for thinking gay men are hitting on them. Basically, you are denying science when you say that's not what you're doing, which makes you as dumb as those people who say MMR shots cause autism and then are shocked when there's a measles outbreak."

"So, you're saying if I tell people gay guys hit on me, there's going to be a measles outbreak and I'm autistic?"

"One hundred percent . . . also, none of this means you have an inkling of what it feels like to be a woman."

I put a piece of delicious and exotic uni in my mouth and savor my victory.

"Okay, look." Oh, God, he isn't done yet?! "So you're telling me the old guy at my gym who puts his foot up on the bench in the locker room and blow-dries his balls *while staring at me* isn't hitting on me?"

"Wait." I accidentally inhale the uni and for a moment it's like a tongue on the back of my tongue. "What?"

James nods and leans into the table, lowering his voice. He knows he has me now. What he doesn't know is that it's taken him three times as long as it should have to reach this red-alert, ball-drying information.

"Is there grunting?" I ask. "I'm imagining grunting."

His face squishes up in disgust, like a pet just sneakily farted nearby. "Kelly, that isn't relevant."

"No, seriously, I need to know."

"There is no grunting."

"How can he not grunt?!"

"Why would he grunt?"

"What kind of powder does he use? Like, baby powder?"

"Yes."

"A giant bottle?"

"Personal size."

"Is he hairy?"

"No."

"Do balls really get that sweaty? Do balls keep sweating after you exercise?"

I remember the first time I inspected a pair of balls. I have no idea which boyfriend it was or when, but the saint let me watch the skin move and retract around them and I remember yelling, "It's like a nipple skin bag!" Basically, I'm a dream girlfriend and now I'm a dream wife, and so, after exhausting a few more important scientific and cosmetic questions, I return to the matter at hand.

"James, I don't think that has anything to do with you or him hitting on you . . ."

"Kelly . . ."

"He's just a normal, hairless dude, powdering his balls. He just wants dry balls, who the heck wouldn't?"

"But he's staring at me while he does it."

"Well, obviously, you're staring back at him!"

"I'm not."

"Then how do you know he's looking?"

"I sneak glances."

Check, please.

IT'S EARLY, BUT THE kids are at school, and I'm in my pajamas alone at home when I get a text from James.

"He's asked me to go to the smoothie place with him after I'm done working out."

I text back, "Who?"

I get an emoji of two cherries.

I text back, "Agent Cooper?"

James replies, "The guy who isn't hitting on me with the powder balls. Powder ball guy. We talked, he actually seems pretty cool."

"Cool. Go have a smoothie with him." I'm glib. I don't even take a moment to think before I text a person back, I just type. Especially when trying to enjoy my alone time in the house.

James is so bad at flirting. I've watched women flirt with

him at parties for years and he never knows what the hell is going on. Maybe this guy *is* hitting on him. Slowly I'm changing my mind from *James is being a stupid straight guy who thinks he's being hit on* to *Oh, there is a good chance this guy is hitting on him. I mean, smoothies?*

But if I'm being truly honest with myself, do I really care if this powder ball guy is hitting on him? Curious, yes. Care, no . . . I mean, James seems totally straight. If he suddenly had a hankering for perfectly dry balls, then God bless him. I would be fine with it. Truly. Because 1.) I do not have balls to offer. And 2.) I am very open-minded. I may even walk them down the aisle when they get married. It's a love story!

There, I've convinced myself the guy is totally and absolutely hitting on James. Oops.

I get a text.

"Can you pick up the kids later? We may hang out for a while."

As wonderful as having a house to yourself can be, I'm not sure anything beats spying on your husband while he's on a date with a man who makes a display of powdering his balls.

I walk around an H&M store, casually trying to find a great spot to see them exit the gym. My heart rate is now up, just like the time I came here for the H&M/Isabel Marant collaboration. Only this time I'm not standing outside a change room in sequin leggings asking my friends, "Is this too much of a look?" This time I'm here to get a look. After fifteen minutes of avoiding salespeople and trying to look blasé as I skulk around the store, I finally spot James exiting the gym, and beside him is powder ball guy. My husband is on a date.

PBG was not what I expected. He was taller than James, probably six foot three, muscular, burly, and totally bald and shiny, which made me instantly think about his powdered, wrinkly nutsack.

"They're cute." A young, extremely thin, gaysian H&M salesperson stopped beside me to spy on PBG and James, too.

"You think they look good together?" I ask as I lean against a table, mindlessly stroking the fifty percent acrylic sweaters like they are cats.

"They're really cute. Especially the bearded one," he says, matter-of-factly. I stop touching the sweaters, realizing they could foreshadow my old-spinster future, with no husband and a million cats.

"Really?"

James is the one with the beard. Maybe gay men really do like him. He does have girl eyes and eyelashes.

Salesman nods, and straightens the cat sweaters I was stroking. "He's adorbs."

I watch James laughing as he listens to the animated PBG talking to him.

PBG stops walking, James stops walking. I duck, thinking they've somehow caught me.

The gaysian salesman grabs his chest. "Are you okay?"

"Yeah!" I say, standing back up.

"I thought you were shot with a stun gun. You just dropped."

"Why would you think that?" I ask, still looking at PGB, who looks around and then leans into James and whispers something. James barely reacts but I can tell he is thinking.

"I watched *Taken* this morning. Sorry."

They stand together, talking in the middle of a crowd. I'm suddenly seeing my husband as part of a beautiful male couple.

"What are they doing?"

"Who?" The salesperson turns, sees James and PBG, and knows exactly who I'm talking about.

"They're talking, why?" he says. Shifting his weight from one foot to the other, the salesman looks down at my hand now clawing the sweater. This spinster–cat-lady thing is becoming real.

"I don't know." Oh, I do know, but I can't tell him I've sent my husband on a date. I'd like to, but my anxiety forbids me from looking ill-prepared and crazy to a person in retail sales. I know how fast these stories spread. I worked in retail!

"Is there anything you need help with? A sweater in your size?" I quickly release the now sweaty, man-made material, which was most likely improperly sewn by children in Bangladesh. Fuck it.

"That's my husband," I say, and the salesman takes a moment to register what I'm saying. His hand comes to his mouth as he gasps and looks outside at James and PBG and then back at me. "Oh my God!"

"What?"

"This is tragic. Did you know?"

"No." I laugh, trying to appear like I have my shit together. "That's just a new friend of his. He asked my husband to go for a smoothie with him, so I told him he should." Maybe if I tell him this, he will agree, rather than continue to believe they are a couple?

Rightfully, the salesman looks confused. "You sent your husband on a date with a hot guy? I mean, your husband is way hotter, which sort of makes this crazier. Are you crazy?"

My shit is no longer together. "Oh, yes, actually I am totally crazy."

"Wait, is your husband the bald one or the one with the beard?"

"Beard."

"I thought so. He has gay face."

"Wait. That's rude."

"Sorry, it's true."

"I mean, it's rude to the LGBT community, it's a terrible term."

"I'm gay, I can use it. Like how black people can use the N-word."

Ew. When someone says "the N-word," I start to sweat. I hate it, and I'm already in here sweating.

I'm really impressed that I'm this uncomfortable in an H&M and I'm not even in a changing room.

"He's pretty," I agree, looking to the door, planning my breakaway, not sure where I will go.

"I didn't say he was pretty."

"Okay, that's also kind of rude." Clearly I have no idea

what "gay face" is but now I've engaged on a higher level with this guy and need to get away from him.

"Can you have gay face and be straight?" I ask.

"Um, no, not really . . . maybe."

From another part of the store, someone calls this terribly certain prophet of gayness to the front registers. He turns to me, not realizing the complete confusion he's leaving me in. "If you need help, give me a shout. Good luck?"

I turn and catch James and PBG entering the smoothie shop. James is holding the door for him, continually smiling with his pretty gay face.

I have two options here: force myself to go home, or be myself and enter the smoothie shop and meet this guy my husband has seen naked and seems to suddenly like.

I choose the latter because I am drawn to pain and suffering, I hate forcing myself to do anything, and everyone should always be themselves.

James and PBG are in the corner of the shop and James's back is to me, which is perfect because I'm not much of a spy and had no plan for what I'd do if he saw me when I walked in.

I take the table across from them, my back to his, and I listen.

James: "So then the guy just grabbed me and put me in a headlock and it hurt, but I didn't want to look weak."

PBG: "Of course not."

The "Of course not" came from a very rugged grumbly voice box. PBG's voice was way sexier than my voice, which is actually really annoying. My voice is one of those voices that make people say, "Oh, I didn't think you'd sound like that." Which is *not* something you say about a voice you envy. Mine is borderline grating, and I know this, because I sound like my mother and my sister.

Oh, God, now what are they talking about?

PBG: "You don't count. You're fine just the way you are."

What the hell is he talking about, James is fine just the way he is??

I hold myself back from interrupting the conversation. James said he knew what it was like to be a girl. Does he need this hot guy to save him now? To lift his self-esteem so that they can make out later? I mean, when he texted he seemed unsure about this smoothie date and now, hiding alone from this table, it sounds as though he's being smooth-talked.

PBG: "I've seen how well your body has changed over the last few months. The lifts are definitely helping."

That's it. I turn and poke James in the back.

"*Hi!!* I thought I heard your voice!"

James turns slowly to face me with a look of shock on his face that I'd seen only once before—but on all three men, when on Christmas day my dad took over Henry's remote-control plane and accidentally and immediately crashed it into the side of his house. James is in a similar confused state of extreme shock. I try to appear as casual as possible.

"What's going on?" he asks. I have no idea where I'm going from here. I'd gone off script, the sound of PBG's sexy voice, the compliments about James's new hot gym bod, the thought of my gay-faced husband on a date . . . it all just set me off.

"Uh . . ." I stammer, picking up a drink from their table, sip it casually, simultaneously realizing that this was a very awkward move on my part. Not smooth like PBG's balls, not at all. Especially if it wasn't James's drink.

"Well, you said you might be here, so I thought, maybe I should come, too. Here I am. I'm here."

"Oh."

"Yeah, you know me, I'm a fun *wife*." *Oh my God, Kelly, shut up.* "I wanted to surprise you for lunch, so I'm here! Hi!" I can't stop myself, I want to but I can't. I turn to PBG, "I'm Kelly, James's wife." Oh, God, I feel it, I can't stop talking, my words are coming out uncontrollably like the boulder in *Raiders of the Lost Ark*. But not the one in the Indiana Jones ride at Disneyland, because that ride is always broken (yes, even after having been closed for repairs forever).

PBG smiles at me; his teeth are better than mine and his smile is so much better than mine. "Nice to meet you. I'm Joel."

"Joel, cool name. It's common but you really don't meet many. I'm James's wife. Hey, babe, what are you drinking?"

I called him babe, I called him babe, I called him babe. "I dunno," he says, "Acai?"

"This is fucking, fucking delicious. Shit. It's good." Wow. I'm really going for it now.

"So good. Mmm, I *love* acai. Joel, do you love acai? I love everything about it except how it's spelled, A-C-A-I, but sounds like Ahh Sigh Ee?"

Yes, it has happened, I feel I've lost my mind. I'm doing what anxiety types call disassociating and going into what James and I like to call robot talk.

I'm full throttle into the I'm-here-for-a-reason-I-can't-disclose-so-I'm-going-to-talk-out-my-ass version of robot talk. I'm like a kid with a 500-word essay who is talking out of her ass. Now would be a better time for Spock talk, where I don't show any emotion and have zero tells. That would at least have prevented everyone in this entire smoothie place from turning to look at us, because my voice is now ringing loudly with a very weird metallic edge.

I shift forward and put my hand on James's shoulder. I don't even want to but just can't help myself; I'm letting this ball-blowing Joel guy know I own James. I once heard the phrase, "She's pissing all over him. Marking territory." That is what I am now doing to James, peeing on him with my body. This somehow calms me down, giving me a false sense of hope that James will no longer be dumbfounded by my presence, and I refuse to give him another chance to question why I'm here. He knows why I'm here! He's cheating on me with the powder ball guy.

"So, what were you guys talking about? I couldn't help but overhear and wonder what you meant by James is just fine the way he is?" My breaths are short and shallow. Looking at Joel's meaty hands, I see the hands of a lumberjack. He's the definition of burly. A hairless, burly man. He is everything I will never be.

Joel swallows his mouthful of white coconut milk or almond juice or something gross. "Oh, right, I was just saying he's not gay obese."

"Gay obese!?" I shout.

"Yeah." Joel laughs, the laugh of someone who knows exactly how hot he is—his teeth must have set him back twelve grand. I've always been proud that my teeth cost my parents nothing, mostly because we were a family of great taste but little wealth and I was proud that I could pitch in where I could. But now I wish I had veneers or at minimum a Zoom whitening kit, because my teeth were ugly and basically the West Hollywood equivalent of chicken nuggets.

"Gay obese. It's just, like, five pounds thinner than a thin straight guy. It's a joke." He laughs at me while looking at James, like I'm an outsider. Like I'm a long receipt from CVS that you hate so much and have to stuff *somewhere* but have no idea where to stuff it! Like I'm some flea-ridden dog on the side of the highway and a BMW is passing with one of those blue French bulldogs that cost five thousand dollars looking at me out the window. I'M NOT A FLEA-RIDDEN BITCH, DO YOU HEAR ME?!

"Look, I know you have a crush on my husband because he has gay face, the guy in H&M told me about it, but he's straight. James, James is totally straight. We fuck!" I was like a machine gun hitting the floor and discharging.

James shoots me a look and starts laughing.

"We could fuck more."

"What!" I'm not even sure what is happening here. Am I upset? No. Am I jealous? Of PBG's teeth? *Yes.* Am I feeling like a crazy person? *Of course.*

KELLY OXFORD

"I'm sorry I said that, that was really weird."

Joel sets his smoothie down on the metal table and looks at me with his big brown eyes, sexier than bin Laden's bedroom eyes. "I don't have a crush on your husband," he says matter-of-factly, with the body language of Joan Crawford and the face of an MMA athlete—I can't name one, as I don't care about MMA.

"James has a crush on me."

James looks at Joel, confused. "Wait. What?"

Joel tilts his head, like a dog listening for clues. "Um, then . . . and Kelly, I'm really sorry you have to hear this"—I nod for him to continue, absolutely filled with glee at what I know is coming next—"then why do you look at me when I'm—drying off?"

James laughs, in a very friendly way, he laughs very hard and yells, *"No, man. You're staring at me."*

Okay. Maybe James is now experiencing what it's like to be a woman. I don't think a lot of men have this conversation. Straight men with women, yes. Women go through this sort of mix-up on the daily, with men assuming they like them. I mean, not while blow-drying balls or anything. But, like, on the bus, maybe a woman will look at a guy and a guy will assume she is interested in him. Or those times when a woman finds herself in the section for yeast infection creams and looks up into the rounded mirror and a guy is looking over from the prescription-waiting area at the same time and he comes over and insists he knows you and needs your number.

"Okay. Wait. Before we get into this, I'd like to know

what was happening outside. Before you came in here you were very close."

"You were watching us before we came in here?" PBG asks.

"Of course I was! Since we're all being so honest right now, I should just tell you that I was, in fact spying on you from inside the H&M with a gaysian salesperson and he thought you were a couple. For a minute, we held our breaths like kids at Disneyland waiting to see Aladdin kiss Jasmine in the now defunct *Aladdin* show. I literally thought you two might kiss."

James looks like he wants to die. I don't blame him.

I wouldn't blame him if he left me and flew off on the wings of a gay unicorn at this very moment. Just, like, lifted up into the West Hollywood sky on a fucking rainbow while spraying glitter on everyone below. Why would he even want me, a natural-toothed crazy girl, over this bulky man who powders his exceedingly dry nutsack? I hadn't even waxed in a month.

Joel very sexily chimes in, "I was trying to make an ex jealous."

I reject that claim.

"Joel, you look at James when you blow-dry your balls and powder them; James, you look at Joel when he is blow-drying his balls and powdering them."

"Okay." James is standing up, he's leaving, I've pushed him over the edge.

"Wait, wait. Let's just stop talking about who is looking at whose balls."

Joel raises his hand. "I've never seen James's balls, he is very discreet."

"They're great." I smile. "And I really appreciate that you're hairless and powder your balls. I wish I had your spirited initiative. You're basically the lionheart of grooming and appearance."

On the way to the car James pats me on the shoulder and I imagine I'm in a magical parking lot in a new dimension where I haven't embarrassed him.

"Why did you tell me to go for a smoothie with him? It's not like I wanted to hang out with him. It was your idea!"

"I don't really understand what happened. One minute I was just trying to luxuriate in my peaceful, quiet house and the next I was sussing out feelings of whether or not I would be cool about your newfound fluid sexuality! I am a very open-minded and curious person who just so happens to suffer from debilitating anxiety. I lost it!"

"You were jealous? That's cute. You know I've been in locker rooms my whole life and I never ever look at other dudes, right? It's just natural not to look."

"I mean, but you knew he powdered them. You can understand my confusion. You're claiming not to look, but then offer me up this uniquely Joel thing that happens in the gym."

"I wouldn't call it unique. I think there might be a better word to describe it."

"Okay, we can stop now."

I steer him to the left.

"My car is over here. I guess it doesn't matter if he liked

you or not, in the end. He's the one who thought you had the crush. You're stuck with me. Unless, of course, we have another rough patch again and you want to leave me or I leave you, which is fine. Can't keep a caged bird, or whatever."

"It's really cute when you show that you care this much." He hugs me too tight.

"Oh my God, get off of me! Stop touching me. I can't breathe."

Later that night, I poured a bubble bath and lit some candles. I needed an Oprah moment. I felt terrible about my behavior, and I relived it all in the tub. Maybe some scenes are better played out in your head. Maybe you should think before you text. Maybe you should trust your husband's obvious heterosexuality. Maybe you don't always have to cause a scene so stupid that you insist your husband change gyms.

I dry almost completely off, put my foot on the edge of the tub, and call James's name.

James comes around the corner, I flip the blow-dryer on, point it at my crotch, and say, "I'm looking directly at you."

And one day I will tell my kids' friends, "Sometimes you just have to flip on a hair dryer and point it at your crotch while looking at your husband. If you're up for it, that's the sort of thing that keeps marriages together."

Good Guy Gone

In a scene we've played out many times over the course of our lives up until that moment, Lauren, Josh, Adam, and I tumble from the backseat of John's car onto the icy sidewalk in front of the house. There is only a slight wind, but in the dark, we stand so close that I gently bump into the bundled bodies around me, the frozen air stinging my cheeks. I love the winters here because I know they are dangerous. The local weather report is full of fun facts like, "It's minus thirty-seven degrees, your skin will freeze in less than ten seconds today." Living on the edge is what we Canadians do.

John Binder shouts, "Hey-oh!" up to the house where his wife, Brenda, is opening the front door, "Hey-oh!" she returns, quieter and higher-pitched; they are like birds calling to each other. The Binders are our family's touchstone in terms of our family friends. The Binders are the family that we are happiest to be around, and so, we are around them weekly, sometimes daily. Spending time with them is the same as ordering in Chinese on a night no one wants to cook. A relief.

"Hey-oh!" is how my parents' friend John always greets us and everyone else. It is so casual and island-like, it doesn't fit what John wears: a nice brown hat with a short feather in it and a long dark winter coat. This greeting, it feels totally out of place in our gridlike, vastly open, land- and snow-locked city. "Hey-oh!" answering the phone, "Hey-oh!" answering the door, "Hey-oh!" walking up to a service person and amiably gaining their attention. It makes more sense to say something like that in the summer; yeah, "Hey-oh" is definitely a summer greeting.

John's greeting is his very own, meaning, no one else does it, or does it quite like him. This greeting is so individual and commanding of happy attention, it's like he's Santa Claus or the mayor of a super-laid-back town, and it always makes me feel like I'm part of his own chill guy parade when I hear it.

"Ohhhh. It's coooold. Hurry up, you guys, get inside, we have supper ready." Brenda giggles. Her giggle sounds like

Betty Rubble's. "Hope you're hungry!" Still giggling, she quickly shuts the door to keep out the deadly frozen air. There is real frost decorating the windows, at least three feet, climbing its way up to the roof, and through it I can see my mom and Brenda now setting the table for a big family meal. They have no idea that we'd spent the last half hour of our trip with our dads to the Muttart Conservatory not looking at the plants or the waterfall but stuffing ourselves full of ice cream.

Dads are less concerned about the correlation between sugar and children acting like assholes, so they let us eat it with reckless abandon, with zero thought given to how being hopped up on that sweet kid-crack is a direct antecedent to getting into a heap of trouble.

I never really know who starts any sort of trouble when it comes to Josh and me. I mean, except for the time when we were four, and I decided we should play doctor. His job was to catch the doll that was going to "fall out of my vagina." That was definitely my fault. Brenda and my mom knew it was my fault because Josh didn't know anything about where babies came from, whereas my mom had taught me how to draw the female reproductive system by the age of four. But, you know, I think the world should actually shoulder some of the blame for this whole "playing doctor" notion. It's someone's fault for putting that idea into my head and every other kid in the world's head. It's the fault of the people who complain about kids playing doctor. By so doing, they are informing us that there is such a thing to begin with, and that it is something

KELLY OXFORD

that adults complain about and therefore an interesting game.

Getting into trouble is not a skill that our younger siblings possess. Our mothers describe Adam and Lauren as "sweet children," while Josh and I are described as "shit disturbers" and "little shits." Our siblings are only two years younger than we are, but Josh and I are eleven and manage to take that age gap and crank it right open to expose all of their younger-minded vulnerabilities. We rely on their trusting naïveté when we tell them we will eventually let them play Nintendo with us, and on their young illiteracy when we tell them the rules to board games (we totally make them up so they lose). We are wolves and our siblings are little, bitty, dumb sheep. Like twisted wardens with prisoners, or prisoners with rookie journalists, Josh and I use our siblings as tools for our own demented amusement.

"Stop!" Lauren yells. I have my mittened hands on her waist. I push her from behind, as she glides in her giant moon boots down the icy sidewalk. Josh follows suit, pushing Adam the same way. Neither one fights back, stiffening up instead. They are the agreeable siblings, the ones who would never fight back. They are the human version of those PVC pipe learn-to-skate things that kids use at the ice rink. My dad, a giant Burt Reynolds mustache in a large sheepskin coat, gets out of the car, balancing himself on the icy road while he holds on to the passenger-side door. I know we only have about ten more seconds of sibling-torture bliss before he shouts at us to stop.

John turns and catches us. He sees Adam and Lauren,

their frail little bodies bending at the waist, making quick fliplike motions to maintain balance. John laughs because that's what guys who say "Hey-oh!" do instead of getting angry. "Okay, okay." His laugh lilts upward, and then he says slowly, "Stop before someone gets hurt." I like that he doesn't raise his voice, he just speaks more slowly. It's oddly more persuasive.

At the dinner table, John drives his little white robot up to us with a Coke on his tray. Their family has a robot and I am losing my mind as I take my can of Coke from the tiny robot tray. John and Brenda buy all of the stuff my parents never buy. Their house smells of fancy bread that makes any human with a sense of smell feel instantly at ease. It looks like the inside of a tchotchke gift shop, kids' toys strewn throughout, complete with a dog named Pee-Wee and a white cat named Christie. They even have a water-bed. It is kid heaven. But the only thing I ever remember my mom commenting on in their house is a small Picasso print on the wall outside of Adam's room. I mean, of all the great stuff they have, that's what she notices. Their house has *everything*. My house has two rooms in it that I'm not even allowed to play in, and we are not rich! Don't get me wrong, my mother has impeccable taste and our bedrooms are a mess, but that's just why I'm so charmed by watching others live so seemingly carefree, in a house that is full of animals, kids, and . . . well, stuff.

Lauren, Josh, Adam, and I finish our dinner quickly and head down to the basement. The basement is where kids go to disappear. I can't imagine a family not having a basement.

It is where kids gets shipped out of sight and sound, totally unsupervised, while parents get to drink and pretend like they aren't even parents at all! Basements and parental happiness are integrally connected. And the Binders' house is one of the only places I ever see my parents drink. They are much more relaxed at the Binders' house than they are at home. The bond between these four is strong, and decades old. It is like they all become the best version of themselves when they are together. Or, at least to me, my parents become the best versions of themselves around Brenda and John. It is so much fun to witness. John and my mom are the loud ones; they always sound like they are arguing but they are usually just doing something benign like working out how to pronounce Thích Nhất Hạnh without sounding stupid, or trying to remember the rules of Risk. Dad and Brenda are more stubborn and definitely the "enforcer" parents, but Brenda will let you have two Flintstones vitamins if you ask, so she's really a pushover underneath.

The parents play games, watch games, talk, and drink, a lot. John is a liquor rep, so the booze is plentiful at his house. It is all around, and in unusual ways, too. We all have Smirnoff towels, Bailey's hats. Josh and Adam are probably the only kids in town who wear promotional clothing from liquor companies to school.

As thrilled as I am to be in the main level of the Binders' bungalow, the basement brings me a completely different, more intense kind of joy. It is a no-parent zone and therefore more amazing than anything the parented area can offer. There's a wall down there covered in photographic mountain landscape wallpaper of the Swiss Alps, which just screams adventure and risk-taking interior design choices. There are two large fish tanks on either side of a beer stein–laden fireplace mantel, a computer, a TV with cable, and a VCR. There is every movie you could think of, every toy you've ever seen in Toys "R" Us, a live tortoise, a dark and mysterious room off the bathroom that Josh and I call Hell to scare Lauren and Adam, John's office, and last but not least, Josh's bedroom. He's got the basement bedroom, which contains the ultimate possession, coveted by every kid who ever lived in the 1980s, thanks to a movie series and several news stories: Josh has a piranha. For real. I'm shocked that I can't put my finger in the tank for a split second and can barely watch as Josh does it. Having a piranha in your bedroom is like having a pit of quicksand in your yard. It's unheard of. Amazing. It's magic. It could only happen at the Binders' house, where they were so agreeable to pets!

"What are you guys up to?" John asks, coming down the carpeted stairwell in his puffy pants, red Smirnoff sweatshirt, and necklace composed of a few beads on either side of a deer antler tip strung on a leather cord. It was some manly shit, and distinguished him as a member of the mysterious Royal Order of the Horn, a spiritual club from Seba Beach. John started this club with his friends; people who were honorable and very respectful of the lake were offered the chance to join. I don't know what it involved, it seemed to be spiritual things around the fire, the teepee, on the boat, up the creek, or out at Coal Point. I had heard John singing Native American chant types of things before, but I didn't dare ask. I loved a mystery. I also love my dad, though he did not wear puffy pants or alcohol-logo sweat-shirts (he wore nice sweaters and button-ups) and did not chant or have a Royal Order of the Horn necklace.

"We're watching TV." I lie and look down inside the ce-ramic beer stein in my hands that contains a fish from the fish tank but no water. It is flopping around in there, in desperate agony.

"Hey, John, where's the tortoise?" I'd noticed it wasn't in the tank earlier, while deciding I would scoop a fish into a beer stein so I could smell it.

"He escaped," John singsongs, as he wags his finger the way he always wags his finger when he's being spiritual, philosophical, funny, or telling you where to fish for the best fish. "Ahhh, he's around." He chuckles. "A tortoise needs a walkabout. He'll be back when he's satisfied." That's our John. So. Chill. I can only imagine what my father's reaction would be if I had a pet tortoise that went for a "walkabout." Actually, I can't imagine. We don't have any pets. The doorbell rings upstairs and Pee-Wee goes mental. *"Hey-oh!"* John sings as he heads back up the stairs to the parents and the drinks. I take a quick whiff of the fish in the stein.

"Oof." I sharply exhale out my nose, trying to force every algae-tainted molecule back into the air. "Hey, Josh, you wanna smell?" I hold the mustard-colored stein out to him. Josh pauses Super Mario Bros. 3 and looks up at me indifferently, like he sniffs the fish in his tank all the time. But he tips the stein in my hands toward his face, stares at the inky wiggle at the bottom, leans in, and takes a deep whiff.

"Nasty!" he screams, laughing, and pushes the stein back at me.

I couldn't be happier than I am in this moment. I am with my sister, a tortoise on a walkabout, and my friends, in that wonderland of a basement, with my parents and their friends upstairs laughing and truly enjoying themselves, everything in the world safe, happy, comfortable. I dump the fish back into the tank and slump down onto the old couch under the Swiss flowers on the mountainside and watch Mario raccoon-whip his tail around, taking flight.

IT'S 11:00 P.M. AND I'm having a panic attack in bed. I have no idea why. I worry for a moment that maybe I have a clot in my lung. I turn to James, on my left.

"You okay?" he asks, when he sees the blank stare I'm giving him.

"I don't know. I feel no urge to inhale. It's very odd. It's like I'm forcing air into collapsed lungs." James turns on his table lamp, grabs his iPhone, and shifts up on his pillows. I stare at the ceiling, trying to relax and forget about the strange feeling in my lungs, but the second I do, I find myself not breathing at all.

James takes my pulse.

"Well, your pulse is really fast. Do you have pain in your chest?" I shake my head no. "Do you feel light-headed?"

"I don't think so. I mean, I'm not moving at all and my head is on a pillow, so maybe I am light-headed and I don't know it."

"Kelly, I don't think it's a collapsed clot. I think it's a panic attack."

I have been stressed out about my work, but not any more stressed than I usually am. I can't think of anything else that would cause a panic attack. I guess when you're as naturally anxious as I am, it's just the luck of the night sometimes.

"Okay," I say, "good night. I'll just trust that I'm not going to die in my sleep, that my lungs will take over and breathe for me."

"Sure." He yawns. Not being an anxious person, James doesn't know how much even saying those words out loud to him stressed me out.

"If I die tonight, tell the kids I love them and get them into grief therapy for children right away, okay?"

"Yep."

"I mean it. Find the best grief therapist for kids. Promise me you will."

"I swear, I will."

"Busy and Sarah will help with that. Do-you-hear-me? Busy and Sarah will know what therapists are best for the kids."

The next morning James lets me sleep in. By sleep in, I mean till 8:30 a.m. The kids have the week off for Thanksgiving and I hear James watching a movie with them in the living room. I realize I didn't even notice falling back to sleep last night. Ah, I would be good at dying, I think. I would just slip away, no struggle whatsoever. As my mind tumbles down that rabbit hole, my phone chimes with a text from Mom.

"Got a call from Josh Binder. John died last night. He fell off a ladder putting up Christmas lights. So sad."

I read this three times and write back the only word that races through my mind, "No."

Mom writes back, "I just keep sobbing."

My throat begins to close and my eyes rapidly overflow with tears as the information processes through my brain. John Binder is gone? He died putting up Christmas lights? He loved Christmas decorating. There was a Santa and a sleigh and a million big, fat colored lights. He would decorate his house every year, turning it into a beautiful holiday masterpiece. I consider calling my mom at this point but realize it will be impossible to speak. Writing is easier.

I text her. "Where are Brenda, Josh, and Adam?"

She replies, clearly not reading my texts, "I have to get it together to go over there."

"What did Josh tell you?"

My mom doesn't reply. I give her a few minutes, as I sit and cry. I text back, "Hello?" I'm thinking about John excitedly putting up the Christmas lights. How I'd watched him do it so many times. How could he have fallen? Was he alone?

I wonder how my dad is dealing with finding out one of his best friends died, and I text him: "I heard about John."

He replies, "I haven't."

Oh my God, no. I have managed to work myself into the

worst possible scenario. I've sent my father the worst text imaginable. Now I have to call him and I have to be the one to tell him that his best friend is gone. I call my dad, weeping, and it all spills out.

"Dad, I'm so sorry, but John died last night. He was putting up Christmas lights and he fell off the ladder."

Dad shrieks, *"No!"*

"Yes." I cry heavily into the phone. I'm usually ashamed when I cry like this. I have many friends who have never seen me cry, but this cry is completely reckless.

My dad's voice goes deep and quiet, full of anguish. "I was just with him. We were just together and horsing around the other day." Oh, God, my dad said "horsing around" like an old man, like a young boy in the 1950s. This is terrible. This is a man whose heart is breaking, at least I didn't have to hear my mom's heart breaking.

"I'm going to come home for the funeral," I tell him. "I'll bring a kid or two to get us through this."

I get off the phone, still crying, pull back the bed covers, and walk to the front living room, where James, Bea, and Henry are watching *Home Alone*.

"What's wrong?" James asks. He pulls his arm out from cuddling Bea, gets up, and walks over to give me a hug.

"John Binder died last night. Putting up Christmas lights."

James knows that John was a second father to me. The first time I introduced James to my dad (we'd been dating for a few months), John was there, too. I invited John and my dad to meet us at the Black Dog, a neighborhood pub.

"Hey-oh!" John and Dad, both in suits, waved James and me over to the bar.

My dad is a Pisces, and so is James. I wasn't really sure if they would be grumpy with having to meet each other, or chill. John is chill. (James joked that he immediately liked John more.)

"Oh, he has a nice coat on. This is good, Don. Nice coat." John chuckled and gave me a hug.

"Thanks." James smiled and shook my dad's hand.

"You guys are supposed to be at work?" I pointed to the suits.

"Now, now. We *are* working," John said in his wise guru tone, sipping his rye and water and wagging his finger.

He was so open, friendly. He made any situation lighter and everyone comfortable, because John loved life, and now he was the first one in my family to lose his life.

I tell James, "I'm taking the girls with me to Canada. I'm going to miss Thanksgiving this year. You can go to Annie's without us to celebrate."

"But your *Pretty Woman* theme birthday party at the Bev Wilshire?"

"I'm canceling it." I mindlessly wander toward the kitchen, then stop. "When I was a kid, Josh and Adam's tortoise escaped and went missing for months inside the house. They eventually found him behind a couch. Then, as a treat for the tortoise, they put him outside to forage, and there was a freak snowstorm and he died."

Two years ago my dad left my mom. It was not nice, it was not pretty, and it was not easy. When I was a child they were very loving and supportive, but I often wished they would get a divorce. As I grew older I realized that they'd been together for so long they couldn't function very well without each other.

Watching your parents' relationship crumble, as an adult, is very difficult. I would venture to say it's more difficult than being a kid while your parents divorce, but I guess that would depend on the circumstances surrounding the divorce. In my case, it was very difficult to support both of my parents. My dad didn't really want to talk about it, and it was all my mother wanted to talk about. I ended up simply leaving the country. My decision to leave Canada and "test out" the US for a while came at a time when I needed a break from my parents, to let them work out their issues without me. I shut down when the people I love have problems. I am a problem solver; if I can't help, my walls go up and I feel sick. This is because deep down I need everything to be perfect. I need everything to be perfect because deep down I need to feel safe. Order is safety. When I couldn't help things get back in order, I moved to the States. I had the stress of my own marital issues, and three kids. I couldn't parent my parents through their disaster. No matter how much I loved them and felt their pain. And if Dad and Mom divorcing caused the whole family to implode and they never spoke to me again, I could always blame it on distance.

Going back home to face them both, under the circumstances of their best friend's death, is grim. The next day I text my dad, "I know this is very selfish of me to ask, but it would be really nice for Lauren and me if you didn't bring your girlfriend to the funeral. You don't have to listen to me, but I wanted to tell you it would be easier for us. I know it's selfish."

Dad responds, "No, she isn't coming." Lauren and I can't handle that he has a girlfriend who is the same age as my husband. This is all new. Losing John and having to meet this girlfriend all in the same day would cause me to spiral so hard.

WHEN WE GET TO Customs in Canada, they ask Bea, "Are you visiting family here?" She responds, "We're going to a funeral. Maybe he'll be in a box and maybe he won't. We aren't sure yet."

Bea's intrigue with the funeral is palpable. I've told her she's going to have to cool it with the death talk and the questions when we're with the Binders. I've explained that they were very upset that John had died and that Uncle John had died an accidental death.

"Why is that different?"

"Well, if it's a sickness death—"

"Like brain cancer or boob cancer?"

"Yes. When someone dies suddenly, you can't believe it's happened. You don't get to say good-bye or tell them anything you'd want to tell them before they leave. They are just gone. But sometimes you say good-bye and can prepare better for death if it's a sickness death. It's all very sad, though. It's the worst."

"Yeah. That's sad. Passing away is sad. Maybe we shouldn't

tell the story about the ladder in front of Grammy," she says.

Despite the circumstances, I'm excited about bringing the girls home. As difficult as my family has been and as most families are, I still want to be close to them. I want to give my kids some level of the connection and the familiarities that I had; the basements with the Swiss Alps wall and the walkabout tortoise on Friday nights. Grandparents, aunts, uncles, and cousins; I took all of that from them when we moved to California. If my kids had cried, or complained about moving, I doubt we would have gone through with it. They had no issues with leaving Canada, and they all say they want to live in Los Angeles. They love visiting Canada, but often I feel like they don't know what they're missing. They're missing tobogganing until your cheeks freeze. Falling asleep to the sounds of family arguing over politics. Poutine.

My mom picks us up at the airport. It's hard for me to see my mom as a single woman. Bea laughs as we're driving out of the airport parking lot and down the highway. "Oh my God!!!" She's pointing at a truck covered in snow and laughing so hard. "That truck is covered in snow."

"Mom, she doesn't even remember *snow*." Sal laughs, doodling on the window fog like she used to when we lived through winters.

My mom's new house is in a new development. I can't talk about the house a lot, it's a by-product of the divorce, I can't talk about the divorce with either of my parents. Not yet. Not now.

"Mom! This snow is making me feel so *alive*!" It's the first blizzard of the year, there is a heavy snowfall warning, and by morning there are two fresh feet on the ground. Bea's been shoveling outside on my mom's small front deck for over half an hour, still obsessed with dying but now talking about how *alive* she is. "I feel so *alive* out here!" she shouts, putting snow in her mouth. I roll my eyes. Lucky kid. She doesn't yet know the feeling of loss that death really brings.

We go to Brenda's house to see her the night before the funeral. They have a new house I've never been to in the neighborhood they always lived in. No more Swiss Alps wall. I've been away from my hometown for twelve years and I didn't even know why or when they'd moved. It makes me feel lonelier. Neither family is the same.

I'm nervous, walking up the snowy steps in ankle boots that are fit for mild rain in Los Angeles. I want to look up at the roof to see if any lights are up there, but I don't. I look at the ground around the house for signs of John's fall and see nothing but snow. A dog barks to announce we've arrived and Brenda opens the door, the same way she always has, but without the "Hey-oh!" Everything seems off.

Brenda smiles a huge smile but seems smaller; we're all older, she is still beautiful. Making small talk with someone you haven't seen in a few years can be lovely or difficult and this was something in between. We were all happy to be together, but, I think because of the shock, all we can really say about what has happened is, "This is really terrible."

My mom makes everyone tea and she and Sal bring it

to Brenda's front room. Bea digs through the tables and walls full of tchotchkes and pulls out a Monchhichi doll in a Santa costume. "Bea, if you want that you can have it," Brenda says. And she asks me about Los Angeles and I don't really want to talk about it, but I want to take her mind off everything, so I deflect to Sal and how well she's doing in school and Sal takes the conversation over from there for a while before the dog starts to bark at someone who has arrived at the door. It's Josh, with his thirteen-year-old daughter, his six-month-old daughter, and his girlfriend. We haven't seen each other in years and he's suddenly a man and carrying a printer into the living room. Brenda says, "Yesterday was hard. He was cremated yesterday. Now he's at peace." Brenda says she's happy he's at peace and in a better place and I can tell she believes that, and I feel slightly better. She drinks her tea. I walk over to Josh and hug him; he looks over to Sal and Bea. "Well, there's some déjà vu." While Josh's daughter discusses her haircut with Sal ("I look like Ron Weasley, the hair color was a mistake") and Bea plays Monchhichi with the dog ("Don't fall down, Monkey Santa!") Josh sets up the printer and prints out some poems and the letter Brenda has written for the minister to read at the funeral the next morning.

He brings them to her, kneeling beside her chair. She opens the first, and speaks in that stubborn tone of hers I've grown up with. "Nope! Not this one, the word *evil* is in it. I don't want any words like *evil*, nothing negative." She's right.

She reads the next and is satisfied; Josh's girlfriend puts

this one in her bag. My mom bounces the baby on her knee. I realize we should go back to the house and make dinner. It's American Thanksgiving.

My mom fills us with turkey and potatoes and carrots and dressing, my sister doesn't make it over because of the snowstorm, and we all fall asleep early. In what feels like minutes, I awake to Mom whispering into the room I'm sharing with Bea, "It's time to get up."

"Thank you." I open my eyes into the dark and pull myself up to sit. I open the window and see more snow. There are several feet now, reflecting the moon and the streetlights, creating a glow much brighter than an early morning in California. I feel an overwhelming sadness. Today I have to say good-bye to someone who was an enormous part of my life. Today is the first day I will be in a room with both of my parents since my dad left my mom. John and Brenda were not happy that Dad left Mom. They were both disappointed in my father. This fractured their lifelong friendship. I held so tightly to memories of these two men together, my two father figures, caring for us, entertaining us. Knowing that they rarely spoke in the last few years is heartbreaking. My mom told me that John and my dad hadn't spoken very much, but my dad told me he and John were now talking once a week. It sounded like they'd only just started to mend the tear in the bond when John passed away. This idea killed me. The idea that both of my parents were mourning and would not speak to each other was also painful to process. The pain of knowing that John and Brenda, who'd devoted their lives to one another, were now forever apart, was unbearable. Nothing was the same. Nothing would ever be the same. It felt like the child in me was dying, too. And it's my birthday.

I wake up Bea.

"I get to wear all black today!"

"You can wear all black whenever you want, Bea." She is excited to go to the funeral, to see her grandad, to see people cry. I walk into Sal's room. She is dressed and asks me, "Are you okay? Happy birthday?" I blow air from my mouth in a whistle. "Nope, but love you for asking, let's go."

We drive very slowly over the ice-covered streets and through tall snowbanks, beside cars undulating billowy clouds from tailpipes, from the edge to the heart of the city where the big red church stands. We don't talk, my mom, my daughters, and I. And when I enter the church, I see everyone from my childhood and teen years, transformed. It is the part of the movie where the actors have donned gray wigs and fat suits and wrinkles were added and noses and ears had all grown. My mom takes her time parking the car. She is probably preparing herself to deal with the funeral and seeing my father. Like me, under normal circumstances she is very sensitive. A miscommunication with a salesperson will put her over the edge for hours. I get it and I do not envy how she must feel. Two women stand near the door, they hug and cry very loudly for a few seconds in their tight knit dresses. By the time we pass them they're done. The back hall of the church is full of early attendees. We enter the "quiet room" and see Brenda surrounded by her closest family members. She stands up when she sees us.

"Oh, good, you're here, where's Gaye?"

I hug her. "She's parking the car."

"I want all of you to sit up front."

"Okay." I nod. Family members crowd around us and I manage to sidestep out of the room with the girls.

Churches don't bother me. I find them relaxing the same way I find hospitals relaxing—they all have this institutional aspect, with rules, formality, the little old ladies who come in to set up the coffee and tea. Every church has them. They are here today.

"Grandad!" Bea yells when she sees my dad, and runs to him with Sal. He is wearing his nicest dark suit and his eyes look both happy to see his granddaughters and crushed at the same time. His body language betrays him, though. It is not only sad, but also slow and old. He hugs the girls and then me. I have never seen my father more devastated.

"Happy birthday, babe. Can't believe it was over thirty-five years ago that the doctor told me I couldn't deny you."

"And yet you aren't embarrassed it was because I was born with your unibrow."

"Your mother around?" My brief moment of levity vanishes, turning to anxiety in an instant.

"When we left her, she was parking the car."

"Okay, I'm going to the bathroom. I'm going to stay out of her way."

"Whatever."

Just as Dad leaves the hallway, Mom exits the "quiet room" and tells us, "Lauren is in the church with Craig."

I see my sister and hug Craig, her soon-to-be ex-husband. Lauren's eyes are puffy from crying. "This is just the worst." The six of us sit in the third row.

I lean over to my mom. "Mom, Brenda wanted you with her in the front row."

My mom shakes her head, no. I know her well enough to drop the subject.

We sit and wait while the crowd gathers. My parents' friends Eric and Joanne sit with my father three pews behind us.

"Grandad should be with us, but he isn't because of the divorce," Bea says, judgmentally, under her breath. Children see the truth and say it. It is a blessing and a curse. A few months ago my sister told me that Craig left her. This would have been the perfect time to tell Bea and Sal that divorce doesn't have to be as bad as it has been for my parents, their grandparents. Craig and Lauren sit side by side, they still work together. They are friends. If we weren't at the funeral I would have gladly taken this opportunity to show my daughters that people can end their marriages more amicably than Grandad and Grammy have. But the girls don't know that their aunt and uncle are waiting for the divorce papers. And now is not the time. I'll save that dose of reality for later. This moment is enough reality for them right now. And for me.

At the front of the church, on a table, is a photo of John

in his brown hat. His necklace with the beads and the deer antler tip is also there. The minister brings in the urn.

Bea crawls onto my lap and touches my chin. She brings my face to hers and whispers, pointing at the urn, "Is your uncle in there?"

"Yes."

"Whoa."

The funeral itself is full of songs and crying and well-told stories. Brenda's letter to John was the hardest for me to hear. It started with the story of their being teenagers in love, and with their first apartment, next door to my dad, and my dad's collection of six-toed cats. I'd heard so much about those cats. Our parents were young, in their twenties, when we were born. As a kid, I'd overheard so many conversations between them and Brenda and John—about drinking, and while they were drinking, about those cats, all the silly things they had done together as kids. They laughed so much together because really, they were still kids themselves.

I am crying silently in the pew, wiping my tears with a tissue. Bea looks up at me from my lap and then down again. And suddenly she begins to cry. To fake cry, actually. My tears abruptly stop, which annoys me because I'd finally let go. But in a way it is sweet that she wants to be like me. She's processing grief? I look at Lauren, who mouths, "Is she fake crying?"

I nod. Bea takes my tissue and fake blows her nose.

After the service, Lauren and I stand with the girls and

Josh and Adam. During the eulogy, Adam recalled the perfect image of his dad showing up at the beach in his work hat and work clothes, and how he'd drive down the hill to the beach house, get out of the car, take off his watch, switch the work hat out for a straw one, and put on his Speedo. Not a moment to lose when you love life.

Here, at the reception, Adam tells me he was terrified of me as a kid, that I was Cruella de Vil and put terrible ideas into Josh's head. Even though Josh was the one who taught me how to throw pitchforks at pigeons and how to build throwing-star bombs, I recall, again, the time with the doll falling out of my vagina and I take responsibility for Josh's bad behavior. It feels like the least I can do today.

We sit at a table in the back of the reception. I saw all of the men from the Royal Order of the Horn, John's spiritual brothers from the lake. I never asked them what they do together. To each other, they are basically the old-men versions of the kids from *Stand by Me*. They all grew up together, blood brothers. They are brothers.

I see my dad on the other side of the room and I am both sad for him and angry that he left my mom. We should be together today.

There's a slide show, with photos of John's life. None of them are the memories I have; there are no photos of the time we were in a tug-of-war match against other kids at Fort Edmonton Park and John jumped in and took the end of our rope so that we could win, though unfairly. No photos of him explaining to ten-year-old Josh and me where to catch the fish while wagging his finger at us, then sending us out in the small boat alone. No images of John caroling at Christmas or yelling during a CFL game. No John calming my mom down with a hug when they both got worked up during one of their debates. There aren't any photos of our trip to California, John behind the wheel of the rented van, singing "Sweet Caroline." Eating jalapeños at the San Diego Mexican restaurant to make us laugh, even though he had Crohn's. No John chasing us through Muttart Conservatory on our way to get ice cream. Boat rides through the swamps of Seba Beach, telling us stories about crocodiles and giant dinosaur fish. Making animal sounds as he taught me how to eat crab legs on Vancouver Island. Nothing for the time he brought a box of live lobsters home and we all watched him drop the box in the middle of the linoleum floor and the lobsters went scurrying. There weren't any photos of all of us kids acting terrible and annoying our parents, yet never making John angry. All of the photos did show what a friendly, happy, and thoughtful guy he was. Always in a boat, always with a dog, always with kids. Always wearing a hat. But the photos in my mind were different, those images so drenched with meaning and memories that I'm almost smothered by them.

"I think I'm going to go for a walk," Mom says to me. "Your dad wants to come over here, I can tell." I assume she's being dramatic, but the second she's out of sight, my dad slowly comes to our table and sits down.

"I got you rum in Cuba for your birthday, I didn't bring it here, but I have it, I'll bring it to LA in January," he says, and then turns to talk to Bea.

Sal looks at me, asks, "Why don't we get to grow up with people like the Binders?" then takes a bite of her mini roast beef sandwich. Sal did not mean to out my biggest sadness, the thing I feel most guilty about, on my birthday at a funeral, but she had just done exactly that. We only get one chance with our kids, and the time goes by so fast. Moving to America had in many ways taken away the possibility of having that kind of relationship with another family. We came there too late for James and me to form tight bonds with other parents whose kids were the same age as ours. The lack of a family like the Binders in our lives in Los Angeles is an emptiness that I have always felt. My kids never did, not until today.

"You do. I mean, we have lots of friends with kids that we hang out with."

"None that are my age. None that close to you."

"We can't really have the same thing, Sal. John and Grandad were childhood friends who had kids the same years. Dad and I didn't grow up in the same city, and we both left out hometowns really early." I don't want to say much more. It will only start me on a spiral of different emotions than the ones I'm already feeling.

Bea licks chocolate off her fingers. "Mom? Why is everyone trying not to cry? Are they embarrassed?"

"I guess. You can tell people are doing that?"

She nods, chocolate on her lip. "Look at them."

I already knew what she was saying was true. No one wailed during the service and we all wanted to. It's crazy to say that John was the good kind of glue, the kind that held hundreds of people together, but he was. John made my parents happier. John was the kind of person everyone wanted to be around. I've met thousands of people, none as special as him. No one; and everyone in this room felt the same. All of us were holding back tears, just looking miserable. Puffy red eyes, heads down, hands clenched. We'd just lost a living joy.

"People want to stay strong for each other. They don't want to impose their feelings of sadness onto others. It's cultural. In some parts of the world everyone here would be screaming and it would be normal."

"Weird."

As I am leaving the reception with my mom and the girls, I tell them to go ahead and stop to talk to Josh for a minute. He's standing by the food, holding his baby.

"We'll be at your aunt's house later," I say, trying not to cry. "It's close to my mom's new place."

"Oh, good. How is her new place?"

"It's really nice. Want me to hold her for a second?"

"No, she's my comfort baby."

I smile, happy because I've never held a baby that wasn't mine. I know, I'm weird. My dad tries to sneak by and I touch his arm and stop him.

"Dad, have you talked to Josh?" He doesn't really look up.

"Josh." He's using the same tone he used when he met James, the low control tone. Dad's trying not to cry, just like everyone else. He takes Josh's hand, looks up for a moment, head full of tears; he says, "Sorry." Kisses me quickly on the cheek with a "Happy birthday, see you soon" and walks away, leaving Josh and me together. Dad lost the battle. I'm barely hanging on, and I touch the comfort baby's foot. "He isn't handling this well," I say and look at Josh, realizing I'm speaking for every single one of us.

On the way out the door of the church, I see Sal and Bea standing at the door, waiting for my mom to bring my car around. Bea runs over to me and holds my hand. I look down at the table set up at the entrance of the hall. On it rests John's hat, his Royal Order of the Horn leather necklace, and the condolences book. I touch the feather on the hat, then the necklace. Bea does the same. Then I look over at the condolences book and read, "I remember first meeting John in the 1960s; he came through the door at Dyke's cabin and said 'Hi, I'm John, the good guy.'"

And I cry a flood of tears.

Unplanned Holiday

INTRODUCTION

Me time. A quiet house, to myself. A. HOUSE. TO. MYSELF. How totally luxurious, no kids to warden! Time to reconnect with *me* and ignore *Mom*. Hey, if I'm not happy, they can't be happy. I'll be able to write without interruption. And you know what they say, absence makes the heart grow fonder.

DAY 1

This is a glorious day. I am having a bath and then getting back into bed. No computers.

DAY 2

So, out of nowhere, James came up with the brilliant idea of taking the kids to Canada for almost *a month* of summer break so I can be alone in the house to concentrate on my work! This is a dream.

List of Day's Achievements

1. Ate potato chips for breakfast and didn't have to hide in the broom closet or bathroom while doing so. I just stood in the middle of the kitchen, shoveling the salty crunch into my face hole, in plain view of the cats no less.
2. Decided I don't need to write today, no work at all. It's been too long since I've been alone in my own house. It's been fifteen years, to be exact. I'm barely a grown-up and it's been fifteen years!! I'm just going to do whatever the hell I want! I'm not even wearing a shirt right now. Screw writing more of this entry. Everything is coming up Kelly!

DAY 3

Watched HGTV, topless, all day yesterday, *completely uninter-rupted*. I mean, to the point where the programming began to repeat itself and no one was there to stop me from rewatching it, so I just lay on the couch until 2 a.m. and no one was there to ask me what was wrong with me or to tell me to get dressed.

Here are my thoughts on HGTV. Pretty good stuff, though I really hate it when they show people purchasing cheap and/or ugly houses. Don't get me wrong, it's great when it's a renovation show, I love seeing a house being gutted by clients who aren't really prepped well for the camera. But they could definitely lose these "First house" shows, it's really depressing. They're so excited for their first shitty house, their first stupid mortgages. I don't want to see reality. I want to see the show about the people who buy islands!

Anyhow, that was yesterday. This morning, I've made a list of things I'm going to do while James and the kids are gone this month: WORK, go to a movie, eat the food I want, drink when I want. I'm doing this in front of HGTV.

DAY 4

This morning, I woke up, promptly burped the taste of BBQ potato chips, and realized I need to buy food. I've been on a diet that is exclusively chips, toast, cheese, cheese-toast, and cereal for the last two days.

I went grocery shopping today, on what can only be described as a "hide your purchases on the grocery conveyor in shame" haul of a dozen doughnuts, a dozen microwave dinners, four bags of potato chips (if you buy two you basically get two for free with your value card, please stop judging me while you read this), a few bottles of wine, and some berries (berries are the healthiest of fruits, I tell myself). Look, my kids are gone, I'm free, and I don't want to waste any of this glorious freedom slaving in a kitchen.

DAY 5

I've started feeling guilty about not doing any work, so I'm going to learn how to do a pike position dive and impress the kids when they come back. I watched a few videos today and it doesn't seem too hard.

I'm really sick of the couples on *Love It or List It* (a show where you have to choose between selling your newly renovated old house and buying a new house, or living in your newly renovated old house) who are barely holding on to their marriages, gritting teeth, and obviously on their fourth take of "I don't like this color at all!" and haggling with this lady about what renovations to let go of when she finds out their foundation is cracked. I hate them.

DAY 6

Half a bag of chips down the mouth hole, and drinking a bottle of wine.

DAY 7

I am sick to my stomach. I wonder if there were worms or a parasite in the frozen pork microwave dinner thing I ate?

I've heard that the Coke-soaked pork video where the worms come out of the raw pork are real, and also I've heard they are fake, so I'm not biased in the form of creating my own paranoia here. Legit, something was wrong with that frozen entrée! Within fifteen minutes of eating that thing, my stomach was making the sounds of an obese man getting out of his Cadillac.

DAY 8

I've done nothing. I woke up with some heaviness in my chest over it. I haven't worked at all. How can time go by so fast when you're just watching TV? Decided to be more active this week, so I got my bathing suit on with the intent of trying to dive, but I hate cold water. How does anyone like cold water? I barely like getting wet.

Another thing I became aware of today when the phone rang and I jumped and the sound of my own voice saying, "Please take me off your call list," surprised me, is this: I haven't seen anyone. I've been alone. I mean, suppose I talked to a few people last week? I nodded to a grocery store clerk who asked if I was having a nice day, and I said "Paper" to her coworker, with my head down as I bought my shame food. So that totally counts, right? I've texted friends. I guess I'm not totally a hermit monster eating garbage food alone while watching TV?

Oh, Sal texted me today and asked what the show was "with Jan and all the blond kids from the '90s" and I was, like, "*The Brady Bunch*?" and she said, "Thanks" and I said,

"That was the '60s!" and she said, "Anything before 2000 is the '90s."

That sent me into a bit of a spiral about age, which fully justified my sitting back down on the couch to regain my sense of self and HGTV, all day, in my bathing suit, and eating an entire bag of chips from the bag, not even from a bowl!

DAY 9

Remembered I had more bottles of wine, drank one.

DAY 10

Ten days have gone by and I feel slightly feral. I woke up and realized I hadn't shit in a few days, you know, since the pork incident. That didn't seem good, so I drank a pot of coffee and went for a brisk walk up and down the hill. Nothing. I drove down to the CVS, made sure no one saw me (got a little nervous about being caught, but not pee nervous, I'm an adult), bought a pack of Marlboro regulars, drove right home. I know smoking is terrible, but I had to do it for the laxative effect. Why not regular laxatives, you ask? You're going to wish you hadn't. The last time I tried laxatives I had such blinding gut pains, I basically thought I was having a toilet baby. I sweated, I needed courtesy flushes, I needed a friend in the bathroom with me while I voided my bottom hole because the pain was so excruciating I thought I might Elvis, right there on the can.

Even though I am completely alone at home, I went outside and hid to smoke one cigarette. One of the cats watched me through the window accusatorily, like I was doing this for joy?! No. I was doing this to poop. And guess what? It worked. No sweat, no pain, no friend needed to spot me on the toilet. Dr. Kelly Oxford.

DAY 11

TRIGGER WARNING: Day 11 is a break-in entry.

Sleepy Hollow to nuclear meltdown in twenty-four hours.

I went to a movie with my friend because I needed human contact. I began to talk to myself earlier this morning. I'd been talking to the cats, but it slowly just turned into me, mumbling about a "time and a place for laminate flooring."

When I got home from the theater, the door was unlocked. I stepped in and heard a door shut. Obviously, I ran out the front door and called the police. And I could barely remember my own house number!

I mean, I just didn't realize how slothful a brain could get after half a month of not challenging it. My brain had been on vacation—Bora Bora, St. Barts, a Sofia Coppola film—and now synapses and adrenaline and glands and hearts and nerves were a firing at one hundred percent. It was a physical, emotional, and mental jolt to my system, much like the reaction of a sleeping cat who's had a bucket of water thrown on it (I swear I've never done that).

"*I don't know my address!*" I held my shaking phone in my shaking hand. "It's 11124! 11024! 10124! Ohhhhh, SHIT!" I ran my numb limbs down the sloped concrete driveway toward the street sign.

"Hold on, I'm going to read my address off the sign. Oh! It *is* 11024! I got it on the second try!" I exclaimed, with the same weird delight that I procured from having on my work desk my soccer trophy for participating in a "mini tournament" in 1983.

A helicopter was here in less than three minutes, and they put the spotlight on me. I raised my hands in the air, praying they wouldn't shoot, but also in the slight hope that this was actually a UFO and I was about to be beamed up, up, and away from HGTV. After a few minutes I lowered my arms; I haven't been working out and they are heavy. I didn't move for fifteen minutes, until the police arrived. They searched my house and found nothing. The back sliding door was unlocked, a pot tipped over.

DAY 12

I didn't sleep at all last night and I have gained four pounds.

DAY 13

I made my friend Orlando come over and watch HGTV with me because I'm scared this robber who didn't rob anything might come back. Orlando was joking that the HGTV "Property Brothers" are lovers, which is really gross, but possible. There *is* something very clinical about them, and I don't necessarily think clinical is a sign of incest, but it's odd.

Also, Orlando says the house smells and I look terrible. Of course I do! My house was just broken into and my family abandoned me.

DAY 14

I opened my computer to work but spent the whole day researching things you can catch from frozen foods. My stomach is still upset. Narrowed it down to a parasite.

I'm not going to even try to figure out how much junk I've eaten to be able to gain weight and have a parasite at the same time, but let's just say it was basically a cartload of frozen foods and a whole aisle of chips.

DAY 15

The kids are going to be back from Canada in a few days, so there really isn't a point in trying to write and get any work done before they get here. I've decided that they can never do this to me again. I'm terrible when I don't have a family to boss me around. I get parasites, I leave houses unlocked for thieves, I become an alcoholic. Really, my family probably saved my life.

DAY 16

I've only slept in my bed, sat on the couch, and used the microwave. The house is so clean.

DAY 17

I threw out the rest of the frozen meals. Even though they were making me sick, I couldn't stop eating them. The Chinese food, the pastas, the pancakes, the bowls . . . all photographed and boxed so perfectly. All so tempting. They're gone. I'm now ordering in. Not sure why I didn't do that to begin with. I guess you can't get rid of the tiny poor person inside of you. I'm not wealthy, I live check to check, but there have always been tiny poor people inside of me. Three of them, actually. And now I support them.

Speaking of, I'm not telling the kids that someone broke into the house while they were gone. Too scary. They can discover it when they read this. Surprise, some weirdo was in your bedroom. That's what you get for abandoning me and going to a glorious cabin in Canada while leaving me here to work and finance your gallivanting!!!!!

DAY 18

I just spent twenty days watching HGTV and gaining weight. I've never been happier to have a family. I'd be so irresponsible and full of parasites without them around to force me to work and fund their every wish and dream.

CONCLUSION

Absence does make the heart grow fonder. This is particularly true when you're a neurotic and *me* time is more work than *them* time. Also? Get checked for parasites.

Dogs Can Never Be Like Kids

Since becoming a parent, I've taken notice of the times people utter some variation of the phrase, "Having a dog is great practice for being a parent." The idea that getting a puppy is anything like bringing a baby into your life makes my insides groan with silent objection. It is a stupid thing to say. Here are but a few of the MILLIONS of reasons why. Let's just get the obvious out of the way: humans adopt puppies when they are usually around eight weeks old. Humans, generally, are responsible for their babies the moment they come out of a vagina. Human babies are useless heaps of flesh and muscle. Human babies cannot sit, they cannot roll, cannot walk, and cannot make a movement of their own conscious accord. A human baby will scratch his eyes out if you don't keep these tiny mittens on them, did you know that? Why doesn't anyone tell us about the self-mutilation and tiny mittens? (Probably because it would squash the never-ending comparison to getting a puppy and having a child.)

The only bodily functions a human baby can manage that are useful on the regular are the mouth and butthole functions. And, truly, they can't control the butthole at all, and the mouth-suction function is just a survival instinct— a human baby will literally latch its mouth on to anything to try to drink milk. You've seen it, a baby trying to latch on to a check or a shirt, they are totally helpless and they are human. So, you basically have to do all the moving for the human baby. Not the butt or mouth stuff, but everything else. That's not like a puppy at all. Puppies can run when they are six weeks old, you dumb people.

Another thing that makes having a puppy different from having a human baby is that human babies do not come with fur; it's your responsibility to constantly regulate their body temperature with clothing and/or blankets. If you have too much clothing on your baby, they lose their minds and cry; if you don't have enough clothing they lose their minds and cry. Babies cannot tell you if they are too cold or too hot. So, unlike baby dogs, they can't walk, sit, go to their food bowl when they're hungry, or regulate their own body temperature. I would frankly love it if my kids had been born able to sit up and walk to a bowlful of kibble, put their faces into that shit, and just eat. I had to put in at least forty-five weeks of nonstop catering to my human babies before they got to that stage. (Not that I fed them kibble, okay?) And then you can't put your baby in a crate and go to the movies and eat delicious movie-theater butter-topped popcorn and Milk Duds. No, a dog cannot prepare you for babies. That is just a ridiculous statement. And people should just stop making it, forever.

But I do believe that a dog can help a person get through the rough transition of *human babies growing up*. Over the past few months I've been witness to my own personal demise in this very regard. My kids are suddenly basically fully functional people and my duties as a mom have suddenly gone from "You are everything. I need you. I love you." to "Drive me. Money. Stay Away." They have become independent of me, and I now find myself clawing at them to regress. I offer to dress my oldest daughter. I'll pop in the bathroom and offer to "really wash" my son's hair while he's in the shower because he can't possibly be doing a good job. And I continue to offer to wipe my six-year-old's butt while she's on the toilet.

These offers are met with the following responses, in order:

"What? Are you kidding me?"

"Mom, get out of here. You are disgusting."

"Are you actually serious?"

It may all sound fucking desperate, but I've just spent *the last fifteen years of my life* providing everything, being responsible for everything from bathing to feeding to clothing for three children, and suddenly . . . suddenly, what? *No one* needs me to ask if they have to pee? *No one* needs me to wipe a nose? No one needs me to fill a water bottle, find a sock. As I watch my youngest, Bea, reaching to the countertop for the Brita water container, master of her own hydration, I pray she knocks her glass over. I visualize, on a loop, her dropping the glass, because I want to hear it break and I want to yell, "Don't move!!" and swoop in with my perfected glass-cleanup system (not trademarked but may as well be, it's so good). But I stand there and watch Bea as she realizes there isn't enough water in the Brita. I watch her successfully fill it up with water, wait for it to filter, pour it into her glass, and I know to the depths of my soul that all of my usefulness is gone.

And now, I'm learning, sadly learning, what comes along with this transition of the kids no longer needing me for all the things I'd changed in my life to learn (like the glass-cleanup technique, which, sure, will still come in handy but hardly at the same rate).

When your children no longer rely on you for basic needs, the dependence they had on you is basically gone. You'd think that would be a huge relief, and of course it is; the healthiest of us want our children to be self-sufficient. But what you don't quite anticipate at all is that your children's brains suddenly tell them to be autonomous from their parents and to become independent thinkers. Without their needing you to do and teach them basic things anymore, you become a hanger-on (*Let's talk about your day!*), a question asker (*What do you think of your new teachers?*), a rule maker (*I don't want you on your phone after 10 p.m.*).

And once the children see you for your uselessness in their day-to-day living, there is no end to how far the uselessness shadow might be cast. My children roll their eyes if I dance to a song I like ("Oh my God, stop"), talk ("Mom, you can't say you love Rihanna, you just can't"), do my makeup ("Why do you bother putting on makeup?"), wear high heels ("Why do you bother dressing up?"), wear sneakers ("Mom, I'm wearing Nikes, you can't"), whistle ("Hahaha, I thought there was a murderer in here"), or breathe ("Mom, can you be a little quieter?").

I have become a joke in my own home and to my own flesh and blood, and it's ruining my self-worth. I don't feel like fathers go through anything as severe as mothers do when it comes to this parental bridge, this crossover from being a needed and life-drainingly depended-upon human being to being a punching bag or, worse, ignored. Because, you know, to kids the relationship remains fairly positive as the child gets older: dads can avoid emotions. Sure, dads love their kids when they are babies and toddlers and continue to do so when they no longer need diapers and strollers. It's just that dads don't wrap up feelings in whether or not they are pushing strollers. Not like women do. I've not only seen this behavior in my children, I've been the perpetrator of it. I was a daughter who grew out of needing a mother for every single thing. When I no longer needed her to fill my toaster slot, she was toast.

In order to deal with my sudden uselessness around my household, I've found myself going out with my girlfriends more and drinking more wine. So, now you know why women drink so much fucking wine, I guess.

Allowing myself to attend every dinner, drinks, party I am invited to has been serving its purpose, in that I'm not at home feeling useless; instead I often find myself staring off drunkenly in the corner of a dark bar, or in a childless friend's yard, wondering what the fuck I'll do next.

I'M CLIMBING UP THE steps of Florence's old Colonial Revival house, when I'm greeted by a thin, European-looking woman with soft, red hair who I am certain is vegan. "The pot bar is in the back on the right, coats can be left in there, too. Enjoy." I smile at her as I step past a full-coated, sleeping Old English sheepdog. It's Florence's birthday, I'm sure she has the marijuana for medical reasons and I'm told Wiz Khalifa's joint roller is playing pharmacist this evening. Why not. Party down. And when I see a gorgeous Middle Eastern woman wearing $100,000 in jewelry, a curve-accentuating Hervé Léger dress, sitting in front of a wall of glass apothecary jars full of pot, I know for certain it's Wiz Khalifa's joint roller.

A birthday party, a reminder that we're all getting older. I guess when you're middle-aged in Los Angeles you get a prescription for pot for genuine health issues. So maybe this pot bar isn't for getting wasted so much as it is for feeling some relief from a bum shoulder, glaucoma (no, seriously, no one under eighty years old should have glaucoma), or degenerative disk disease. From my experience, a lot of smoking pot when you're middle-aged is habit, or due to pain issues or illness, and maybe a bit about getting blazed, but it's a different blazed than what smoking pot at seventeen felt like. At seventeen you're experimenting with limits, by thirty-seven you're well aware of your limits and mostly want to muffle the reality around you, the bad neck, the shitty marriage, the kids ignoring you.

Kanye West's "Ni**as in Paris" is in the air through the house, under the decorative live olive branches and pink roses hanging from the chandelier and over the dining table. Sunny passes me the joint, I take a pull off it, and look at her and moms in the room, blazed out of their minds, dancing to Kanye. Fuck my kids, I don't need them either. This is great. This is the best. This is what it's about. Kanye, weed, and moms. Jen looks at her phone. "My babysitter wants to know if my husband is going out or if he's staying in. She doesn't know what to do. He's on the couch sleeping." She laughs, we all laugh. And as I'm laughing, I realize . . . I mean, this scene is definitely something out of a nightmare my kids might have. I cough. I stop laughing and look at my laughing girlfriends.

Sometimes, it doesn't matter how good the pot that Wiz Khalifa's sexy joint lady in an Hervé Léger dress has given you is, your reality doesn't vanish. I need another way to feel better.

I'm leaving the party when I see Florence again. "Is that your dog, the Old English Sheepdog, behind the gate?"

"Did someone put him behind the gate? That pisses me off."

"Well, the vegan-looking redhead put him back there when the cake came out. Does he go after cake?"

"No. He's fine around food and people."

"Then that really is annoying. Why would she put him behind the gate? He was being really good."

And I suddenly feel it. Familiarity. Rules. We were talking about the dog the same way I usually talk about kids.

I'd never really considered an Old English Sheepdog a real dog you could own. They seemed like fake dogs. The only sheepdogs I'd ever really seen were the dogs from *The Little Mermaid* and *The Shaggy D.A.* I was shocked, after typing *Old English Sheepdog* into Google, to discover that those enormous mops of hair are hypoallergenic and shed-free. I text Florence, "This true? Is your dog hypoallergenic?" Blue text bubble responds, *Yes basically.* It then takes me two seconds to decide I am going to purchase this breed of dog that I'd been blind to my whole life, yet have always loved. It was like suddenly realizing you're in love with your best friend and could possibly spend the rest of your life with them, but the dog version.

I excitedly tell my childless, two-dog sister my plan. "Lauren, I'm going to get an Old English Sheepdog. I didn't know they were basically hypoallergenic and nonshedding." If Google is where I get almost all of my dog information, Lauren is my man on the ground.

"Don't get an Old English Sheepdog. You need to mix it with another breed or it will have health problems. I bet they are mixed with poodles. Anything mixed with a poodle ends in -doodle."

I google *Sheepdogdoodle.* And here, again, is suddenly something that I didn't realize existed, and I want it.

Sheepadoodle puppy (Old English Sheepdog/ Standard Poodle hybrid). *When crossing a Sheepdog with a Poodle, you significantly increase the dog's hypoallergenic factor to (nearly) 100%. The result is a "smarter" Sheepdog and a GREAT family dog. These dogs are eager to please, non-dominant,* intelligent/extremely *trainable and make good companions. They are loyal and very people-oriented and are great with children. These dogs are great with other animals, too! Their calm temperament and love for people is notable. [dogbreedinfo.com]*

Wow, that sounds beyond perfect, so it has to be true! Eager to please, loyal, *extremely trainable,* calm, great with kids and other pets?! I sit back, pillows propped up behind me in bed, and, like a teen finding free porn, scroll through thousands of photos of Sheepadoodles. Instant favorite? The sheepadoodle on the boat, his long coat blowing in the wind, his front paw up and hanging casually over the side of the boat. In my mind, his name is Captain. I text this photo, with the word *Captain,* to several friends. No other reference included. Those closest to me realize this means I'm researching–slash–obsessing over dogs. When I've exhausted all the Google images of Sheepadoodles, I switch to Instagram and search for more photos by searching #Sheepadoodle.

Immediately, I'm drawn to a tiny square image; I touch it and it expands into one of the most incredibly funny dog photos I've ever seen. Perfectly composed, the image is taken looking inside the open window and into the backseat of a black Cadillac. Sitting in the backseat of the Caddy are three tall doodle dogs, looking, very thoughtfully, right at the camera. Like three old-time gangsters, the dogs look out the window, waiting for their afternoon ride in the Cadillac.

I immediately share the photo on Instagram—"This makes me very happy. That doesn't even cut it. Stop. #cardog"—and I tag the account I found it on, which is how you point people in the direction of the original work when using modern technology (this is an important point, as you will soon see), and I drop my phone onto the bed. Spent. Because of my neurosis and constant obsessive self-awareness, I immediately reflect on how sad it is that the moment I shared my new interest with the world I suddenly feel a renewed purpose. I walk out of my room and find one of my kids, to show them the pictures of Sheepadoodles. "These are cute, right?"

"Mom, I don't want to look at dogs," Henry scoffs, looking at Sal; they share a smirk and a head shake commiserating over their dear, sweet, incredibly lame mother.

"What if we get one of these, you guys?" I say, in an up-beat tone, but they don't bite. I try again. "What if we get a dog?"

All three kids suddenly turn and look at me. Now, that is mom crack.

"Really?" Henry asks. He clicks his tongue. "Nah, you're just saying that."

"No. I want one."

And there we go. This has become the best scenario of all time. My kids are again interested in something I'm interested in, and this dog is going to give me something to care for in my house. I will get to pick up its poo, I will get to let it outside, I will pour water for him, and he will look to me for leadership. At the same time, he will provide a bridge between me and my kids, something we can all share and talk about. Two birds. One stone. I'm elated.

Over the next few days I complete my research on Sheepadoodle breeders, I buy books about puppies and dogs, I watch fifty episodes of Cesar Milan, studying all the terrible dog owners he has on as guests. I really can't get over how simple most of these fixes he suggests are. Like, vicious lunging dogs stop lunging when you stop pulling back on the leash? Come on, owners, you need a television show and a soft-talking Latino to tell you this? I wonder how people can own dogs and be so stupid, for about as long as it takes for me to remember that people don't even know how to raise their own children. I'm not perfect, but I fucking try. Note to my children: put that on my grave: *I'm not perfect, but I fucking try.*

A few days later, surely after I've checked again to make sure that no one in the house needs me to weigh in on their shoe sizes, homework, or hydration, I flop onto our teal sectional and open Instagram. Some wonderful human with a love for my old pal, caps lock, has just left me a surprising message in response to my Sheepadoodle post from a few nights ago, "YOU STOLE THIS PHOTO! THESE ARE NOT YOUR DOGS. MY FRIEND TOOK THESE YOU

ARE STEALING FROM HER! TAKE THIS DOWN RIGHT THIS INSTANT," under the picture of the three dogs in the backseat of a Cadillac photo. True, they aren't my dogs, and maybe she is friends with the person who took the picture, but I've done nothing that millions of other Instagram users don't do, EVERY SINGLE DAY, which is share a public photo on my own account. I mean, I even credited her with a tag that led people to her account! What does this woman want from me?! THAT IS WHAT HAPPENS ON THE INTERNET. I mean, she was getting new followers! I hastily type into my phone screen, responding to this PERSON, "I'm not sure what the issue is here? I'm not pretending I took this photo and these are my dogs. People who follow me know I don't have dogs. I credited the person who took this photo. There is no problem here! I'm sharing the love!" And almost immediately I receive another CAPS response, "THESE AREN'T YOUR DOGS. TAKE THIS DOWN! YOU ARE LYING ABOUT TAKING THIS PHOTO!"

This is the moment where the situation has become so absurd that I wonder if this is a friend, pretending to be a person who doesn't understand the Internet at all and probably lives under a rock. I click on the account of the person sending the messages. It's legit, one billion boring photos of one beautiful Goldendoodle. Goldendoodle on the floor, Goldendoodle in the yard, Goldendoodle in another yard, Goldendoodle in the dog park. As much as I wish it were the case, I do not have a friend who would put herself through the torture of setting up this account to play a joke on me.

I respond to this doodle lover, "I did nothing wrong. Welcome to the Internet." Within a minute, all of her doodle comments disappear and I realize it's because she's blocked me. "Great!" I think, "It's over." But, of course, I am a helpless naïve, because my downtime on this doodle crisis is limited to about thirty seconds. That's approximately how long it takes before I receive the following tweets to my account on Twitter:

@kellyoxford THEN you can take pictures of your own dog & not TAKE MY SISTERS PHOTOGRAPHS and call them yours! NO CLASS w NO DOODLE Creepy

@kellyoxford TAKE MY SISTERS PHOTOGRAPH of the 3 doodles IN MY MOTHERS CAR OFF YOUR SITE!!! YOU SAY YOU TOOK IT? HAHAHAHA Creepy very creepy

Wait. No class with no doodle? Did she just say I have NO CLASS WITH NO DOODLE?

Aside from the fact that these posts were accusing me of things I had not done, they were totally insane. I did some online stalking to make sure they weren't coming from a terrorist cell. Nope, just two sisters in their sixties who likely enjoyed an evening of *Jeopardy!* and *Wheel of Fortune,* a cup of Constant Comment, and reading the novels of Patricia Cornwell, with their Sheepadoodles at their feet. They really had no idea what was going on.

This is the point where, if I had a life—if I still had babies to care for instead of children in school solving math problems I'm so glad I don't have to solve—I would have walked away and just lived my very busy life, cleaned up a broken glass or something. But I don't. So instead, I took a screenshot of the tweets about me having "no class and no doodle" and posted them on Instagram with the caption:

How did something so beautiful turn so #creepy

All I did was share and credit a photo on Instagram. Insane.

#NOCLASSWITHNODOODLE

People recognized the insanity immediately:

"Someone needs an Internet 101 class"

#doodlegate2015

"THOSE CAPS ARE INSANE THOUGH."

"You should see the shit they are saying about you on Facebook."

"Is this real life? How is this real? This is hilarious!"

"Someone doesn't get how the Internet works."

"This isn't going to be a *Time* cover or anything."

But for every single person saying exactly what I had been thinking, I was feeling worse and worse. I mean, maybe Doodle Sister really nailed me on having no class and no doodle? Maybe she really hit a nerve. I *was* trying to get a doodle. I had contacted a breeder, and I was on a waiting list. It would be a few months until I had my little bundle of hypoallergenic fur. In the meantime, they were reveling in their doodle joy. I was still doodle-less and dealing with my kids, who were bored by me.

So, like the self-aware person I am, I did check out the kind of stuff they were saying about me on Facebook. It wasn't good. The photographer doodle sister had posted a picture of a piece of pizza, telling me I should steal that instead of pictures of her dogs. Meanwhile, Caps Lock

Doodle had shared my account on her page, asking people to send me messages:

"SHE STEALS MY SISTERS PHOTOGRAPHS SEND HER A MESSAGE, TELL HER TO GET HER OWN LIFE!" and after I blacked out their names, I posted these on Instagram, too. I couldn't help myself. #doodlegate2015 had taken on a life of its own and the comments were rolling in.

"Bahahahahhaaa!

"Bwahahahha!"

"This is priceless!"

"This is an *Onion* article come to life."

"This is why cat people are better."

All I'd wanted was a dog to make me feel needed, like I wasn't a mom joke, and somehow I'd just proven to myself that sometimes, moms just are jokes. By trying to open my life back up again, to fill it up with activity with a dog, what I'd done was fill it up with activity about dogs, that weren't mine, in the most inane and futile way. It was sad, when I thought about it. But I tried not to think about it that much and just laugh at the absurdity of it all.

#Doodlegate lasted weeks, there was fan art, retweets by celebrities, and meanwhile I sat at home, asking my kid if I could wipe her ass, waiting for my doodle to be old enough to come home to me. Then I'd have a doodle. Then I'd have some class.

On Boys and The Body Shop

Lately I've been trying not to procrastinate by going online while I'm in my office. I've unplugged my Wi-Fi. I'm very proud that I only spent one day plugging it back in for thirty to forty-five minutes at a time, lying on the floor with my laptop to get my Redfin, Shopbop, Twitter, and links-I-found-on-Twitter fix. And it is a fix. I have become so OCD about my online routine that I physically feel the clock ticking when I'm not on schedule. This is a very *soft* addiction, perfect for neurotics. The Internet is very good at making all of us feel less alone, but it really is a time-sucking devil for those of us who work on our computers all day. We can lose valuable time getting vacuumed down the rabbit holes of flash sales and buzzfeeds and listicles and clickbaits. We have to "self-regulate" our time. I'm doing to myself and my laptop what I used to do to my children and their iPads. I probably should still regulate my children on their iPads. But I'm too busy trying to regulate myself.

In my time alone, without the Internet, I've truly come to realize the grip that the Internet holds on me. It's like I can't breathe if I haven't done my circuit. So, I had to re-create the circuit somehow, lest I hyperventilate and never get any work done whatsoever. After some trial and error, I created an "office circuit," which consisted of picking some music, listening to my neighbors, looking out the window, and checking out my bookshelf. Maybe I should just confess that I am a professional procrastinator and just get down to work? But who can do that?

On the third day without the Internet I found my diary from middle school on the bookshelf, and from then on, my office circuit became music, look out window, diary. It's a sign. I've given up my online life to work, and here I've discovered the earliest form of self-serving blogs, tumblrs, and tweets known to mankind. The diary.

As it turns out, I used my diary to fully document my obsession with boys. I was completely, one hundred percent preoccupied with boys; a boy-crazy girl. I called them, thought about them all the time, talked about them with my girlfriends nonstop, I lived for boys. One boy took up most of middle school. His name was, of course, Mike.

(All boys in the 1990s were named Mike.)

Good Lord, I was obsessed with him. Reading the thoughts I had at thirteen is awful, and I've had to fully accept that I was a stalker. I mean, a full-on stalker. Mentally unstable. I'm not sure how much of my life was *actually* this focused on the boy, or if my diary was just a spot to vent my frustrations (obsession, rather), but the words on the page paint a portrait that I am less than thrilled to experience today. To wit:

25 FEBRUARY

Mike was really good at the beginning of the day. I thought he had switched locks on me but I had just really forgotten my own. [Wow, great fantasy. Really great, not-psycho, accusation right there.] *I took him out of 3 classes for it! The 3rd time was because I took his bag and jacket and he needed his bag for gym.* [Reader, I stole shit out of his locker.] *Then he changed his padlock!* [No shit, there was a crazy girl pulling him out of class, accusing him of switching her lock, who then stole all of his stuff.] *But in the afternoon he took the note here and read it!* [Note is missing. I can only imagine.] *He got mad, I think. Well on Monday he took this note I wrote about him and it said all this stuff about how much I loved him. It's weird talking with a guy when you know he knows you like him. I really like Mike. I wish he'd feel the same about me.*

27 FEBRUARY

It's over between Mike and me! No, I'm not sad. It's really over unless he wants to change it. Which I doubt. He's ignoring me. I have too much pride to fall into that pit!

[1.) You have no worries about pride. 2.) You and Mike never "started."]

15 APRIL

Well now Mike seems to be showing some definite signs but is still lacking the major ones. Tomorrow I think will be the day, I was going to afterschool today but dream girl was hanging around him, now I hate her even more. Ahhgh!

[I'm sure showing some "definite signs" was a smile or something.]

16 APRIL

Well all the things I heard about Mike liking me weren't true. During class change, I went up to him and asked him if he'd ever give me another chance and he said "well ya when I like you" and I said "so you don't like me" and he said "well ya as a friend" and I said "I guess then what I heard wasn't true." And he asked what I heard and I said "nothing" then we walked away from each other. He left really fast after school.

[I am feeling more and more sorry for this Mike kid.]

APRIL 23

Well today was awesome in the mornin' but towards the after-
noon it got more and more retarded. Well it seems like I'm
writing the same things every BLOODY BLOODY DAY DAY SO
I'LL STOP NOW BYE.

[This is all very true. The next twelve pages of entries,
which add up to three solid months, are basically the same:
me reacting to any attention Mike gave me with "Great day!"
and days where he gave me no attention at all with "The
worst day." But finally:]

8 JULY 2:57PM

My first French kiss. It wasn't as bad as I had imagined.
I really liked it though! Oh yeah it was with Mike ———.
Ooooiiieee F I N A L L Y AFTER ALL OF THIS TIME.

I'll never forget it but I won't write details cuz I don't trust
my family (little sister) even though I know I'll regret it! Oh well
I'm a very happy person. It was definitely worth waiting for!

[I remember this clearly. We were lying side by side on
Penny's basement couch watching *Pretty Woman* on VHS.
During the bath scene, with Roberts covered in bubbles and
singing Prince, Mike rolled on top of me and French-kissed
me. He also pushed his boner into my thigh. To be honest
I wanted to say "ouch," but was too fascinated. The kiss
and boner press lasted but a few seconds. After the movie I
walked him to the attached garage, opened the door, and he
rode off into the dark and rainy afternoon on his BMX, popping a wheelie as he turned the corner.]

22 JULY

FUCK FUCK FUCK FUCK FUCK FUCK FUCK FUCK FUCK FUCK FUCKING SHIT FUCK SHIT FUCK SHIT FUCK SHIT FUCK SHIT FUCK SHITFUCK SHIT FUCK SHIT DAMN SHIT FUCKIN BASTARD ASSHOLE SHIT FUCKIN SHIT FUCK SHIT P O S I T I V E How the hell could this happen to me FUCK FUCK FUCK FUCK FUCK FUCK Now Mike has it too! Shit Shit shit shit Damn damn damn damn FUCK FUCK FUCK FUCK

27 JULY

*He'll get sick. OH GREAT. Mom is making me tell him Oh well I would anyhow. **FUCK** MONONUCLEOSIS.*

[This last one gets me laughing. Not only did I not use the commonly abbreviated term, mono, I bolded the FUCK MONONUCLEOSIS. And how about that flair for language! "Fuck Mononucleosis." I mean, surely I should have known I was destined to become a writer. And the boy obsession leading to such a dismal diagnosis—well, an afterschool special couldn't have plotted a more appropriate outcome. I was like the very embodiment of a hormonal cliché. Thank God I kept this diary. It may come in very handy as my daughters ascend into full-throttle teendom.]

And just like that, a text chime:
"Mom I need to get new clothes." It's my teenager.
The first text is immediately followed by a second.
"Mom, my jeans ripped."

I type back.

"All of your jeans are ripped."

She responds, "No these are my high-waisted ones. They ripped. They aren't supposed to be ripped. Can you come get me from Pizza Guy in an hour? Dad took Bea to the doctor and I want to go to Pizza Guy but I don't have a ride home."

"Fine."

"Thanks!!! Also I need these new jeans before my trip to San Francisco."

Salinger has already made that switch from being my child to being her friends' friend. Our family now comes second to anything else she has going on in her life. She no longer needs me for much more than money and car rides.

Despite my failure to record anything other than my feelings for Mike in my diary, I remember this period in my life very well. My family was a nuisance, their plans always getting in the way of my very important sleepovers or trips to the mall. My friends and I needed plenty of times to obsess together over boys, and when my dad couldn't get me to school early enough for me to walk down to the gas station and have those deep, meaningful, obsessive conversations before the first bell rang, it was the end of my little junior high school world. I remember that sense of needing to be involved with everything that was going on in each of my friend's lives, and I mean everything, and wanting to murder my parents when they kept me from any social event whatsoever. The loudest drunks are groups of sober teenage girls. They think all their jokes are hilarious. All their drama is the biggest deal in the whole wide world. Everything was all boys, and The Body Shop.

Sal had her phase with The Body Shop, too. I could relate to that much, though she had it about a year earlier than I did and this gave me some cause for concern. For at least three years, no one would gift anyone anything other than The Body Shop merchandise. When visiting your friend's house for the first time, you'd get the tour and then the tour of the bathroom to assess her collection of Body Shop products. I can still smell and feel The Body Shop's Japanese washing grains on my fingertips. White Musk, Rose, Peach, or Dewberry perfume oils come flooding back to me as easily as any recent memory could. Sal and her friends appear to have the same obsession, and I find comfort in knowing our transitions from being children who don't know they have ketchup on their face to becoming women came at the cost of body butter and The Body Shop. Sal did not, however, appear to be as obsessed with boys as I was.

I text Sal back. "Maybe I should come on that trip to San Francisco? That would be fun! I've never been." I mean, the boys are going to be there, right? It was time for me to suss this out accurately.

Quick came the response, "Oh my God. Mother, no."

Oh, shit. Was something afoot?

Now that I'm married and no longer have teen boys to stalk, I have become my children's number-one stalker. The younger two are sort of still fine with it, but Salinger doesn't want me around her for too long. It goes along with that thing of her friends being her life. I mean, she needs me to pick her up at Pizza Guy, but she will run to another room if I talk to her too much. I don't even have to make eye contact. "Seat belt on?" She sighs, "Oh my God!" Somehow I manage to act like a complete idiot around her. I'm like that nerdy younger kid the older kids let stick around so they can make fun of him. This is easily done when you don't have the same group logic as the peers.

With Sal, lately, a lot of conversations involve a line of questioning, such as, "Who do you think is hotter? _____ or _____?" and then she texts her friends my answers. Her friends have dozens of snapchats of me saying, "I don't think Harry Styles is hot, I'm not a pedophile." Which is a lie, he's hot. But isn't it worse if I tell her that I think he's hot? I'd rather talk to Sal about Joan Didion or how I think Monica Lewinsky got the rawest of deals. But I've tried those topics, and similar ones, and she doesn't seem as interested in those as she is in my attraction to Harry Styles. Yeah, maybe I do have something to worry about. I'm an idiot.

I turn left off Moorpark and into the flat, desperate parking lot in front of Pizza Guy and text Sal, "I'm here."

She responds, "We're across the street. Sorry. At frozen yogurt place."

I look up from my phone and across Moorpark to another row of sad, small Valley stores. I type, "Is there parking in the back?"

"Yes."

Instead of asking Sal to cross the street and come to me, which would have been far simpler and less annoying for me, I mindlessly drive across Moorpark to Colfax and around the back of the building, where there is an extremely small and crowded, typically LA parking lot. No one here seems to believe enough is enough when it comes to how may cars can fit in a lot.

She isn't standing outside, of course. This is the epitome of selfish kid behavior. I expected her to be in the parking lot, waiting for me. Stupid me, when will I learn.

"I'm outside. Behind the frozen yogurt place that you are standing in," I text.

"Can we give Travis a ride home?"

I pause. Who is Travis? What is happening? I assumed she was with her friend Stella. My curiosity is instantly inflamed. Is Travis her Mike? But I don't want to give Travis a ride home. I don't even want to give Sal a ride home. I'm supposed to be working. I should text, "Of course." That's the healthy parent thing to do, but instead, I tap out, "Where does he live?"

"Close."

"Sure."

I am powerless. I have to know.

In my side mirror I see my daughter, who has wavy, thick hair down to her waist. I didn't have hair that beautiful when I was her age. I once paid to have some Indian lady's hair attached to my head to create the illusion that I had hair that beautiful, but it was just that, an illusion. Sal is much taller than me, and her long legs, bare under her navy-blue uniform skirt, make my legs look stunted, dwarfed. I'm certain children should be better specimens than their parents, otherwise what's the point of any of this procreation business? I'm proud of the traits my husband has passed along—the long legs and thick hair—that heaped improvement on my own genes. Travis trails behind Sal, on crutches. Oh, God, he's on crutches. Mike was on crutches once, it made him so much cuter. This is getting more interesting by the second.

"Mom, we're putting Trav's crutches back here, okay?" I turn and look at her through the car and out the hatchback trunk.

"Sure." Let's keep this mundane, Kelly. All of my "normal" friends who seem "together" and "grounded" claim to have had very boring parents. While I doubt I can ever provide "boring" for my children, I can attempt to be chill.

But she called him Trav.

Sal climbs into the backseat.

"Hey, guys!! Did you have fun?"

My voice does not sound like my own. It is forced like I'm holding in a fart . . . the fart of my desperation to discover Trav and Sal's relationship status.

"Yes." Sal opens her eyes widely and nods, condescendingly, like only a teenager can.

"Hello, I'm Travis," the boy says as he drags himself into the car after Sal. I'm instantly sweating, and panicking a little. He's the same height as her, tall, also has beautiful thick hair, and I will never say this to Sal even though I know she would love to hear it—at her age I would have totally been insanely in love with Travis. Oh my God. Why did I think that? Is that creepy?

Sal and Travis sit silently in the backseat. It's because of me; I know it. I imagine, only minutes before they came out to the car, their happy, loud conversations in the frozen yogurt place. The loudest sober drunks. And now? I've killed their joy. How have I become the killer of fun? When I was in middle school I was the pillar of fun, I was voted Most Talkative Girl, I was voted in as the social organizer for all the school dances and activities.

"So, Travis, you know my name is Kelly, right? You can call me Kelly. I'm very chill."

That was stupid. Maybe that wasn't the best message, so I add an addendum.

"Very chill, but not too chill. You know?"

Travis laughs, and Sal shakes her head, hair getting caught in her seat belt.

"No, Mother."

Oh, God, I got the "mother." This is getting tragic already.

"Where are we going?" I flip over the phone in my lap and tap open the GPS.

"Oh," thick-hair Travis says, "it's just around the corner, on Sarah. I just can't walk that far because of my hip."

If Travis had been my crush I would have romanticized the shit out of this hip thing and this ride home. It would have been a two-page entry, at least.

I pull out of the parking lot and back onto Colfax, then Moorpark, the desolation of the Valley streets comforting.

"I love how dead the Valley is compared to Hollywood," I say a little too loudly.

"Uh-huh," Sal responds, with a tone that lets me know she wants me to shut it, stat.

"Sal, don't you like living on this side of the hill better? There were so many cars and zombie people on the other side, all those cars cluttering up the streets."

I hear nothing from the backseat. Am I killing her? This is pretty cool conversation, if you ask me.

"I mean, your dad and I have talked about how when the big earthquake happens, a *lot* of people are going to die, but all of the people on Hollywood Boulevard are going to survive. They can survive anything, under the worst conditions. They can't catch disease from dirty water, they've become immune. In fact, the people on Hollywood Boulevard are already zombies, just waiting for all hell to break loose. The privileged people who have survived will leave town in their rental helicopters and then the zombies will claim Hollywood and all of its riches for their very own. But we aren't going to have to worry about any of it over here in the Valley. These are the sorts of things married people talk about in bed. Look out! Good times ahead!"

"Okaaaaaaaaaaaay."

They say nothing at all. I drive in silence for a few moments, but I want them to talk, because I really want to get to know Travis.

"What happened to your hip?"

"Dislocated."

"What? Sal, didn't Hannah dislocate her hip, too?"

"Yeah, she did."

"Why are you guys doing old-people things like dislocating hips? That's weird."

Travis's look of confusion probably plays off as me calling him weird; he shrugs his shoulders. "Uhhh . . . sports?"

"Oh, my kids don't really play sports. I mean, it's genetic. I'm not sure I can blame any of them for their lack of interest, Travis. I hated team sports. Do you have brothers and sisters?"

Notice the abrupt subject change. I knew I was headed down a rabbit hole of weirdness here.

"Yes, a younger brother and an older sister."

"That's nice."

Other than his bad hip, Travis appeared to have it all: great hair, athletic, big family. Oh, God. Salinger is probably obsessed with this guy.

"Hey, Travis, are you going on the San Francisco trip with the class?"

"Yes."

Okay, well, now I have to go on this trip. She can't go on this trip alone with hot Travis.

"Heeeeey, so am I!" I say as cheerfully as possible.

"No, you're not, Mom."

I nod. "I should totally go on that trip, Sal. It will be fun!"

Sal sighs, "Mother, you can't go."

"Why?"

"You had to sign up months ago."

"So?"

"It's full."

"There's no way they won't let another parent chaperone come! There is no such thing as full."

"Mom, they can't fit any more parents into the rooms they booked. They are full. Sorry. You can't come."

"This is the house"—Travis points in front of us—"up here with the bike out front." I slow the car and pull up to a ranchlike Valley bungalow, the kind you grew up seeing in commercials and family-centered sitcoms. Putting the car in park, I casually lay my arm across the back of the passenger seat, turn around, and make eye contact with Travis.

"Travis, don't you think I should come on the trip?"

"Mom. Stop!"

"But, all I want to do is eat sourdough and follow you around."

"Too bad, Mom, it's full. You had to sign up months ago."

"She's right." Travis's eyes twinkle when he chimes in, "Parent volunteering was closed forever ago."

He's enjoying this. I love his spunkiness.

"Oh," I laugh, "you guys haven't thought of the most obvious thing, though!" I nearly shout, as *I* realize the most obvious thing.

"I can just go on this trip *on my own*, apart from the school!"

"What? Mom, like a stalker?"

I nod. "Uh, yeah . . . I mean, I have your whole itinerary! Hotel name, what time you leave, where you will visit.

Everything. I'll just go on my own and wear a trench coat and spy on you. You won't even know I'm there!"

"Stooooooop!" She breathes deeply and steps out of the car. "Please open the trunk." I do as she requests and she reaches in to get Travis's crutches. I watch him shut his door and hop away from the car. I try to open the passenger window, but mistakenly open the back window. I leave it open and shout through the back, "Travis, I should totally come to San Francisco, right? I've never even been."

"Sure. Nice meeting you!"

"You too!" I smile.

Sal rolls her eyes, passing flamingo-like Travis his second crutch. He smiles and shrugs. I close the back window and sit alone in the car, watching Sal and Travis pick up an animated conversation. I didn't have a conversation or interaction with a boy, where I wasn't stalking him, until I was in my late teens. I sit and imagine myself going to San Francisco, flying in a few hours before them, standing in the Radisson lobby, waving at Sal as the school group checks in. Or maybe I'd play it cool, hiding behind a pillar and just watching, silently. Or I could find out what floor their rooms are on and book a room across the hall and just jump out when they slide those key cards into their doors. In my head, this is already the best movie ever made. *Troop Beverly Hills*–level hilarity with a dash of mother-daughter bonding. Maybe I save Sal and Travis from some poisonous sourdough, or someone falls overboard on the way to Alcatraz and my superior hand-eye coordination allows me to throw the flailing teenager a life preserver at just the right moment so that it lands in her hands right before she sinks into the choppy bay. I can see it. Where's the popcorn?

"Mom?" I didn't even hear Sal get back into the car. I was lost in the bay.

"Sal, are you in love with him?"

"Mom, no. What is your problem? You are acting insane. Drive. Just drive."

I look over my shoulder and pull away from the curb.

"What? I was just making polite conversation."

"Mom, you were talking like a crazy person." She's waving both her hands around as she talks, like I generally do when I don't have to have my hands on the steering wheel.

"The San Francisco stuff?"

"I mean, San Francisco would have been enough . . . but the zombies, whyyy?"

"Salinger, I was just being polite. I'm sorry if I embarrassed you."

I said that in a way that was supposed to make her feel bad, but I don't think it worked. I pulled over to the curb just as she released a heavy sigh.

"Sal."

She wouldn't turn to me.

"Sal, are you in love with him? Why are you so against me coming to San Francisco? What's going on?" Sal turned and looked me right in the eyes, and I was suddenly scared of her. She was so much more willing to engage with her feelings than I was at her age.

"I'm definitely not in love with him. And I'm telling you, again, you can't come to San Francisco because *it's full for parent volunteers. Full.* Think about how weird it would be if you just showed up, on your own, and stalked us. It's weird, Mom. You're weird."

I pulled my mouth into the corner of itself. "Hmm. You don't think it's sweet, at all, that I want to come on this trip with you? Even as an outsider, on my own dime?"

"No." She looked forward. "You never act weird with Henry."

"Should I?"

"Let's just go home!"

I arrive home and Henry is by himself. He's supposed to be doing his homework. His iPod sits on the coffee table, it chimes, quickly, five times, and I pick it up to see he has SIX HUNDRED new messages. 600. These kids don't have diaries. They have texts.

"Henry?" I shout.

"Yeah?" he shouts back. "I'm doing my homework."

"Henry, what's up with all these messages on your iPod?" Henry turns around the corner of his room and into the hallway. He's made sure his face looks as annoyed and dead as possible, body language dragging.

"Henry, you have, like six hundred messages."

"Yeah, because I'm baller."

"Don't you think this is too much for your brain, getting six hundred messages in a few minutes? Do you want a diary? I found mine from when I was your age, I was a psycho."

"What? Mom, you still are and this is a conversation with, like, twenty kids. It's mostly one-word texts. Like,

Yeah! No! OMG. Like, the last time I texted someone it said, G2G. That means got to go. *Because I'm doing my homework.*"

"I'm really proud that you're home alone and G2G to do your homework. I'm not accusing you of anything!" Henry and I are constantly arguing over nothing. We are both really annoyingly similar in getting emotional immediately. "And I'm not an idiot, you know! I totally know what G2G means." (I had no idea what G2G meant.) "Why don't you take a homework break for five minutes and get on the phone and call the friend you want to talk to the most?" I pick up the cordless phone and hand it to him; he raises his shoulders and phone into the air.

"I don't have any *numbers.* Are you forcing me to stop doing my homework and use the phone?"

Henry sighs, punches a number into the phone, and begins to wander away. He is soon pulling the phone off his ear and walking back to me. "This thing is broken. Listen to it." He passes me the phone, sighing, "Can I text now, please?" I put the phone to my ear and hear a busy signal. He didn't know what a busy signal was.

"Henry, it isn't broken! This sound means his phone is busy, but much more importantly, that he doesn't have Call Waiting!"

"Great. It's busy and it's a she, not a he, *Mom.*" Henry begins typing on his iPod.

Wait, he was calling a girl?

"Henry, are you into girls already?"

He smiles. "All day and all night, son!"

"You're writing to a girl? Maybe don't put things in writing."

"What do you mean?"

"I mean, I had a bad experience with that and I was using paper and pen. There are certain things you could email or text that you won't want people to have when you're sixteen or even next week and maybe you don't want to find them in your office when you're thirty-seven. The phone is just safer for everyone."

He mumbles, "Uh-huh, yeah, got it," then bolts around the corner, and down the hall, shouting, *"The phone's lame! It isn't the nineties, no one likes the phone!"*

"THE PHONE IS AMAZING WHEN YOU'RE A KID, AND NO ONE HAS YOUR THOUGHTS IN WRITING AND EVERYONE IS DRESSING LIKE THE NINE-TIES AGAIN AND QUIT YELLING THROUGH THE HOUSE!"

Maybe Henry had a point, maybe it wasn't the same anymore? Maybe times really had changed and I needed to shut up.

"Sal? I have to show you something." Sal emerges from her room in all black: black-on-black Converse, black jeans, black sweatshirt. "I have something for you to read."

"Oh, God, what?" I can tell she's had just about enough of me for one day. I can tell she's expecting me to show her some escape plan her dad and I have created for how to manage the zombie apocalypse or something. I'm a nutcase to my child right now. I've got to take hold of this situation. I have to show her how much more mature she is than I was at her age. I think it will help her understand the insanity I provide her today. I motion for her to sit on the end of my bed and I hold out my diary.

"Your kid *diary*? Oh my God. Oh my God." It is even worse than she thought. Sal hyperventilates over the navy-blue-cloth-covered diary I've just passed to her. Then, she pauses.

"This cover is so pretty."

"I dog-eared the pages to read. Go for it. I was almost exactly your age. Thirteen going on fourteen." Sal looks at the diary page and laughs. "I can barely read this."

"Sal, it isn't that bad."

"No"—she laughs and flips through the pages—"it's cursive handwriting. We weren't taught cursive. Hold on, I'll try." Knowing that my teenage daughter sees cursive writing as some sort of witch's tool makes me sad. Sal's reading of the entry is very stilted and slow, due to the cursive writing only, I'm sure.

" 'Six November. Well since I last wrote, alot [*sic*] happend [*sic*]. After Tom said he'd go out with me after he dumped Melanie, he went out with Moira! Ha, I *was* so mad then. Well since then I've liked Mike! But I found out what they did during *Sleeping with the Enemy*.' " She pauses. "What does that even mean? I can barely read these words."

"I remember it clearly, I was in the hallway, by the ice cream machines, and June told me that Mike dry-humped her and French-kissed her during *Sleeping with the Enemy*!"

Sal snaps her body and leans back. "What? Mom. Gross!"

I continue. "And, weirdly, I chose another Julia Roberts movie to watch the day I made out with him."

"You *made out with him*?"

"Sure. And I gave him mono."

She clears her throat and continues to try to read. " 'I don't know what to do! If things go good with Tom tomorrow (oh yeah Moira dumped him Hee Hee!) then I'll go for him, but if Mike and June brake [*sic*] up then I won't know what to do! Yikes! Yikes! Yikes! Now that we've found love what am I gonna doooo with it?' " Sal pauses and stares at me.

"It's a Heavy D & the Boyz lyric. Okay?"

" 'Ps: Joe and Priscilla are still going out. I think they've done it.'

"Um, Mom? I'm going to need to read all of this."

"You can't read all of it. I mean, maybe you can. There is a through line and the characters all stay the same. It is like the worst young adult novel you could imagine."

"Okay"—Sal clears her throat—"why is *Aimee likes Roddy* highlighted?"

"It was important, obviously."

She continues.

" 'Eight November. Today just to see what would happen I asked out Tom. He said that right now he doesn't want a relationship. Tuesday he'll probably be going out with Nicole! Aimee likes Roddy. Only I know! She decided that today! Becca and I are getting him a present tomorrow (oops I mean Tuesday the 12th). It was my idea! I'm sooooo brilliant! We're gonna get it from the Body Shop' "—Sal stops reading and pounds her chest over her heart with one fist, "Body Shop." Then she continues.

" 'Won't he be surprised! Hee! Hee! Hee! Run to the toilet before I go pee . . . ' " WAIT. Mom, what?" She's laughing. "Mom, I have to read all of this."

I'm touched that she finds my teen years so entertaining, but I want to make sure of something.

"Sal. Do you know why I gave this to you to read? I need to know something. Are you as boy crazy as I was?"

"Um, no! Not at all."

"Not even a little bit?"

"Mom, no, you were totally insane."

"Well, yes, I was. And that's why I worry about you, you know? You are my kid. And I want to be a part of your life. But I don't want you to obsess over boys like I did. I was miserable. So today has been my weird way of gauging how boy miserable you have been."

"Uh, yeah. Mom, you're next-level obsessing in this diary. I don't think there are many people who could match that level of mania."

"Maybe you could. I mean, we share genes."

But my daughter is so different from me. She isn't obsessing over boys and relationships. Maybe she is just obsessing boys in bands. I really don't know how to approach her about safety or teach her anything at all, really, when she seems to make far fewer mistakes than I ever did.

"Are you sure I can't stalk you in San Francisco? I'm fun."

Sal hugs me, I hug her back.

"Mom? You're nuts."

"I'll buy you new jeans."

"I love you."

#NotOkay: The Day My Outrage Went Viral

"I *usually* work from home, in my bed, because it's the most comfortable chair of all, and I generally find it quiet and relaxing. Sometimes I work in cafés, but the problem with doing that is listening to people plan their driving routes through Los Angeles. However, doing that is somehow *more* relaxing than *listening to the howls of my cats, demanding that I let them in and out of the house!*"

I'm talking to my cats; one wants in, the other wants out.

"Goddamn cats." I get up, cross the room, and open the door onto the deck.

"Great, Gertie, come in. Gus, you go out. Let's do this again in fifteen minutes, shall we?"

They pass through my legs in opposite directions, rubbing layers of Persian hair onto my jeans. "*Eew!* Don't pet me. I'm a human, you beasts. You don't pet me, I pet you!"

Today is a *normal* day; I'm working from home and I'm in my bed.

A half hour ago, I turned the television to CNN, but I put it on mute. I never work with the TV on. If being a writer feels like a Sunday night in fifth grade with homework you know you'll never finish before bedtime, then being a writer with the TV on feels like being a fifth grader whose teacher is going to come in and scold you for not doing your homework and for watching too much TV. Nevertheless, I've chosen to have CNN, the HGTV of news (everyone watches mindlessly), as my background visuals today. It's almost like fate. This is as wild and crazy as I get, and it feels good to break one of my own tiny rules.

On the screen I see silent footage of Billy Bush and Donald Trump. Billy Bush has made a career trading off his last name and, in my opinion, pretending to be a journalist. He is full of bumptious self-satisfaction, and he and Donald Trump fit the mold of privileged white male perfectly. They also, from their apparent actions on the screen, seem to have some kind of high-fiving bromance going on that, frankly, turns my stomach. Their smug faces give me the impression that this breaking news is going to add another layer to the dislike I've always felt for both of them.

It is October 2016 and Donald Trump is currently running for President of the United States as the candidate for the GOP. (As an aside, as a Canadian I had to look up what GOP stood for. Gotta say, I had a pretty good laugh over that one.) To many people inhabiting planet Earth, and all the people I know, this feels like a huge, horrible joke. Donald J. Trump is an American icon, a caricature of a capitalistic, chauvinist, science-hating bully. Canadians like to joke about the Ugly American and the Ugly American *is* Donald Trump. If he were to become President, our joke about ugly Americans would no longer be funny. Our collective Canadian prayer throughout this campaign season has been "Please do not take our joke away."

With a great sense of dread I unmute the television. What I hear is Trump and Billy Bush having an off-camera conversation with hot mics. They are on an *Access Hollywood* tour bus. Why does *Access Hollywood* have a tour bus, you ask? Who knows? For some people, this show passes as deep cultural reporting I guess? Or Billy Bush and his pals need a place to pee when they aren't out in the crowds or interviewing soap stars? This exchange was captured in 2005. Many of you will remember it, but because we should never forget it I'm repeating it here word for word:

TRUMP: "I moved on her. Actually, she was down on Palm Beach. I moved on her and I failed. I'll admit it. I did try and fuck her. She was married."

BUSH: "That's huge news."

TRUMP: "Nancy [O'Dell, former cohost of *Access Hollywood*], no this was . . . and I moved on her. Very heavily. In fact, I took her out furniture shopping. She wanted to get some furniture. I said 'I'll show you where they have some nice furniture.' I took her . . . I moved on her like a bitch. I couldn't get there and she was married. And all of a sudden I see her. She's now got the big phony tits and she's totally changed her look."

BUSH: "Sheesh, your girl's hot as shit. In the purple."

TRUMP: "Whoa! Yes! Whoa!"

BUSH: "Yes! The Donald has scored. Whoa, my man! It better not be the publicist. No, it's her, it's . . ."

TRUMP: "Yeah that's her in the gold. I better use some Tic Tacs just in case I start kissing her. You know, I'm automatically attracted to beautiful . . . I just start kissing them. It's like a magnet. Just kiss. I don't even wait. And when you're a star they let you do it. You can do anything."

BUSH: "Whatever you want."

TRUMP: "Grab them by the pussy. You can do anything."

Oh my God. There it is, the conversation that stopped millions of women cold.

I grew up in the '80s and '90s. My parents raised me to believe I could be anything I wanted to be. They even bought me books that said, "A girl can be an astronaut!! A girl can be a doctor, just like a boy!" When I became a parent, I read this book to my daughter, and she asked, "Why couldn't a girl be an astronaut or a doctor? What does this book mean?" I put the book in storage, and I took note. I was telling my child she could be as successful as a boy when she had no idea boys had an advantage. The world had changed a lot since I was a girl.

"You should go to university. The kind of man you want will want to marry a woman with a deep education." This was advice from my well-meaning mother, and I considered this was possibly true, overlooking the fact that the subtext was: *Go to school to get a man. The smart woman gets proposed to by the right man.* I was raised on the objectification of women through a dialogue that was positive and even encouraging, by a feminist, no less!

Even so, the ideas around appearances were still out there, and I studied them like a PhD candidate. All in all, those boiled down to: Have long hair, be thin with a nice bust and hips. Don't have too many opinions and be a good listener.

Objectification. It is a hot, loaded word. Women have been bearing the weight of this behavior forever. But here were Donald Trump and Billy Bush taking objectification to a shocking next step. They were actually joking about sexually assaulting women. Billy's horrendous laughter in response to Donald's remarks put my head in an extreme place. I immediately open my Twitter account and see *everyone* tweeting about this. This is huge. This leaked tape is demanding a response. I have to jump in. I have no choice. Through a pit in my stomach, I tweet, *"Grab them by the p—y," Trump says. "You can do anything." And Billy Bush is like, OK!—This is rape culture. This is what we hear & live.*

My tweet is instantly being retweeted, but I feel like what I wrote isn't as clear as I want it to be. So I tweet again.

Billy Bush cackling after Donald Trump says "Grab them by the pussy. You can do anything." Is rape culture.

I read these two tweets and wonder if I should delete one. No, they're different. I sigh deeply and look back at the television, watching Donald and Billy Bush now shaking hands with a blond actress.

Just minutes before, the conversation between Billy and Trump had turned to this woman, who clearly turned the Donald on. To wit:

> **TRUMP:** Grab them by the pussy. You can do anything.
> *[CROSSTALK AND CHUCKLING]*
> **UNIDENTIFIED VOICE:** Yeah those legs, all I can see is the legs.
> **TRUMP:** Oh, it looks good.

This was the woman Trump just said "*It* looks good" about. It. He called a woman IT. You know how when you get bad news, or you are hit with a flash of sudden pain, it feels like time stops? Time stopped. I'm engulfed in a feeling, a sensation. My body is drowning in it. That feeling is white-hot rage.

Billy Bush encourages the actress to kiss Trump on the cheek.

Fuck this.

"Grab them by the pussy."

Fuck this.

My hands are shaking.

Fuck this.

I've been the "it" in that equation too many times.

I'm taking these fuckers down.

WINTER 1989

I've been waiting for today all week.

1. It's Friday. Schwing!
2. I'm going to my friend Penny's house after school. She lives in a suburb, which is exciting. New houses, so fancy! I live in the inner city. Old houses, gross! We are taking the city bus, which is also very exciting. Taking city transportation is the closest I get to feeling like a kid living in New York City.
3. My crush Mike lives close to Penny, and he too will be on the bus. I will get to spy on him. Schwing!

"Penny!! Let's go." I puff clouds from my mouth into the air, grabbing her arm and sprinting for the bus. It's one of the coldest days of the year. Penny zips her backpack and tries to keep up.

"We're going to slip, we don't have to run."

"I won't slip, I have Sorels on! My mom got them on sale! Hold on to me."

I shift my bag off my shoulder and onto the other so Penny has space to grab, a "dad trick" that always works for me.

"Hold on tight!" I drag her in her Doc Martens across the ice-covered sidewalk. I pray this is the closest I'll ever get to being in the Iditarod, or a dad.

"Shit, Kel, the bus is going to be so full. Let's get the next one." I look to see what Penny is staring at; up ahead of us the number 47 bus has an epic line of middle school kids scrambling to getting on. I spot my crush Mike, he's ascending the bus stairs with his white-blond hair, like a wintry Viking child-god.

"We can't wait! We will freeze to death!"

"We can wait in the Circle K."

"Penny, hold on tight. We're getting on that bus. He's on it."

"Who?"

"Mike!!"

"Kelly, he's dating Gabby. Stop obsessing."

"No *way*. Gabby isn't on the bus. Don't you get it? I'm not missing this opportunity. We are getting on that bus."

I have done my hair today, in a ponytail with teased

bangs. I even used hair spray, enough hair spray that this Iditarod run is barely causing my vertical hair wall to lose a single strand from its crisp wave.

My mom had no idea I'd added the hair spray to our grocery pile.

"I guess you're a teenager now," she said when she found me in the bathroom, backcombing my bangs, hair spray bottle sideways in my mouth. It was a small moment, and a minor one, but my mother was acknowledging me becoming a woman. I was trying to look beautiful, on my own, without her help.

I dig the Sorels deep into the crusty snow on the edge of the sidewalk and double my pace, keeping Penny and her slippery Docs on the ice of the sidewalk, dragging her behind me.

"Hey!!" I hear a girl's voice yell, and I turn so quickly that my cheek is stung by the air.

"Hahaha!" Penny laughs at the *boy* she'd actually run into. He is still trying to stabilize himself on the ice.

"I could have cracked my head, bitches."

He straightens his jacket and I turn, laughing, toward Penny.

"His voice hasn't even cracked yet, and he's worried about his skull?"

I was not a nice tween.

I stop dragging Penny as we reach the crowd of kids piling up into the bus. She nods in agreement.

"That guy is the bitch. He's definitely pubeless. He probably has the penis of a seven-year-old."

Neither were my friends.

"Penny, that's gross." I laugh, of course.

She squints her enviable aqua-colored eyes at me. "A half roll of Certs."

We walk up the two bus steps to the driver, and I pull my mitten, smelling and tasting of old spit, off with my teeth as I scan the bus for Mike. All I see are faces of people I don't have crushes on. The bus is packed, all the way to the back. With my naked hand I fumble around in my jacket pocket for my bus change. My glasses fog up.

"Please hurry, we have to go!" The bus driver yells at me as I blindly dump all the coins I have into his little money box and grab my ticket.

"Penny, I can't see." She grabs my shoulder as we move down the aisle. Penny has a bus pass and doesn't get yelled at. I need to get a fucking bus pass, they're only, like, fifteen dollars for students. My parents would rather pick me up than let me take public transport. They think I'm too young, the pains of being the oldest child.

I remove my glasses and stand in a puddle of sandy melted slush on the bus floor, holding the pole. Other students, adults, are all around and pressing into us. I feel alive with my cement bangs, glasses off, on public transport.

"I don't see him, Kel. Are you sure he got on the bus? Gum?" Penny offers a piece of gum but it's too close to my face and my eyes cross as someone bumps into my butt. I hope Mike didn't see my eyes cross. I put on an annoyed face to counter the cross-eyed idiot face. I'm bumped into again.

"Penny, I can't see shit without my glasses. This bus is too steamy." I put my glasses back on because steamy glasses are less embarrassing than crossed eyes.

"Oh, man," she giggles, "Mike is gonna see you and—"

And then everything goes silent. Those bumps into my butt were a hand and now that hand is crawling from my butt to my vagina on the outside of my pants. And then, the hand is there.

When I was a kid I would jump into the lake and stay underwater, just for the moment when things would go silent. I'd surface, let the yelling, talking, dog barking back into my ears, the sound of my feet as I ran down the hollow wooden boards of our dock. Then I'd hang airborne for a moment before hitting the water again. The loud rush into my ears, then numb silence. I lived for that lonely numb silence in this womblike peace and safety.

But now the tiny invisible soft hairs on my arms and neck stand on end because instead of the peace I felt in that silence, it is fear I now feel. I turn and face a small old Indian man sitting on the bench behind me and pulling his hand back from touching me. He smiles.

"Kelly. Kelly," Penny says.

I'm out of the water.

"Sorry," I say too loudly. Penny is looking toward the back of the bus.

"Look. Look. It's Mike. He's with some guy I've never seen before. Do you know who that is?" I see Mike and feel nothing. I shake my head no. Penny keeps talking. The bus keeps driving. Eventually, we get off and walk to her house. We have dinner, we listen to music, we talk about how Lindsay's dad always says he is going to come see her and he never shows up at the airport. The next morning, my mom picks me up.

"You have fun?"

"Yes."

I get home, go upstairs, and throw the hair spray in the garbage.

I SHAKE AS I type.

Women: tweet me your first assaults. They aren't just stats. I'll go first:

Old man on city bus grabs my "pussy" and smiles at me. I'm 12.

I send the tweet and go to the kitchen for water. My throat is so dry. If no one responds, I'll delete that tweet. It was too presumptuous. I'm asking too much

At age twelve I didn't tell anyone about the Indian man on the bus, because I was embarrassed. Why was I embarrassed? Because it's my vagina. Because that's private? Because I was twelve and I was embarrassed and didn't want to ruin my sleepover at Penny's?

My water glass is overflowing in the fridge dispenser. I take a long sip.

It was the hair. I was trying to look attractive to Mike. I purposefully wanted Mike's attention, I tried to be pretty for him. Maybe my shame was in trying to look pretty. I looked so pretty that a stranger felt he could touch me.

"Grab them by the pussy." I shiver all over, feeling sick

as I return to my room. The video of Trump and Billy on the bus is on repeat. I decide to delete my tweet, but when I check my responses there are too many to count. Stories are coming in faster than I can read them. What is happening?

- *My stepfather sexually abused me from when I was 4–17, no one believed me, I have felt guilty and ashamed my whole life.*
- *Age 7 at toy store, bend down to see Barbie, man reaches under my dress. I go home and bury the ribbon I had in my hair.*
- *Saw doctor for eye irritation and he gave me a breast exam.*
- *I'm laying on my stomach reading, my grandfather puts his hand up my shorts. I was ten.*
- *I'm a secretary to priest. After service he says, "I always wondered what you'd look like with lipstick." Kissed me on lips.*
- *My disgusting music teacher tries to kiss me, I was 12.*
- *I was at a party, 15, smoked a lot of weed and passed out. Woke up to man raping me.*
- *Swimming at busy pool, feel someone reach into my bathing suit crotch and grab me. They swim away.*
- *Space needle elevator with my parents, man behind me rubs my ass. I'm 9.*
- *I was on the x-ray table, tech "adjusted" my pubic bone for 10 mins. I'm 14.*
- *Friend's dad pulled on my swimsuit bottom and looked inside the front. I was 9.*

KELLY OXFORD

- *I'm 5 or 6. Sitter followed me to bed, covered my mouth and put a finger in my vagina.*
- *Grandma's boyfriend put my hand on his penis. She said I lied and bought him a car.*
- *I was gang raped by a group of professional athletes. Guess it was my fault. I was staying in the same hotel.*
- *I'm 11 in hospital waiting room, man waits for my mom to leave then offers me $50 for a blow job.*
- *Family doctor asks mom to leave the room. He then tells me I'm old enough to get a breast exam. I'm 13.*
- *6 years old. Sleeping. Friend's dad spoons me and holds me against my will. I beg him to stop, be he says he knows I like it.*

Those stories all come in in the first ten seconds. Then another four. Another six. This is not stopping. I realize I can't delete my tweet. I have to tweet again. Gertie meows.

"Shut it, Gertie!" I yell.

FALL 1990

"Read the punctuation! Always read the punctuation! O Captain!" from under his gray thick mustache he lets out a tiny gasp. "My Captain!" Another teeny gasp.

Mr. Uzwyshyn is my favorite teacher. I have him for English and Drama, and he makes us all memorize "O Captain! My Captain!" and recite it individually to the class. He has no problem stopping us and making us start over if we do not have enough passion, or if we forget to "read the punctuation." He does not mind spending the whole period making each student recite the same poem over and over, he loves it that much.

"Dave, next time, chest out. More air in those lungs."

My crush, Dave, drops his head, shuffles his feet back under his desk and sits down.

Dave is a little bigger than the other boys, but he's quiet. He doesn't play sports or read Whitman properly. He's complicated, you see.

"All right." The dandruff on Mr. Uzwyshyn's daily black wool sweater uniform bounces to his clap. "There are only fifteen minutes left, so let's watch *Whose Line Is It Anyway?*"

I drag my chair toward the television Mr. U keeps on a tall rolling stand.

Whose Line Is It Anyway? is a British show we watch in both Mr. U's English and Drama classes, where the audience gives an improv team suggestions for different games and the team performs them. He's obsessed with it. Sometimes he laughs so hard he cries, shouts, "Oh, again!" and rewinds the tape to watch the same scene over and over.

I'm also part of the improv groups Mr. U leads during lunch hour. He actually kicked me out of the five-person improv groups, to give other people a chance, because I am always in them. I love improv, I love his class, and I love this room.

Dave pulls his chair up beside mine.

"Hey," he mumbles.

"Hey," I mumble back, trying not to act too excited as

other kids pull their chairs around us. I imagine if we ever dated he would suddenly be talkative, more cheerful.

"I hate 'O Captain! My Captain!' " I say it with the punctuation and my chest out but my joke falls flat.

"I hate this class."

"Me too." My God, I'm such a liar! The lights go out and Mr. Uzwyshyn turns his beloved British television show on.

In the dark, Dave reaches over and lays his hand on my thigh. My body runs cold as I watch his hand skim up my thigh to the crotch of my pants. I drop into the silent pool again. I grab Dave's hand and throw it from my lap.

"You assaulted me." I say it before I realize I've thought it.

Dave laughs.

"Is there a problem?" Mr. Uzwyshyn asks, as I stand up and rush out of the room into the bright fluorescent light ricocheting off the tiled floors and shiny green lockers. I'm breathing fast as I slam open the door into the pink cinderblock bathroom.

"Hey, Kelly. Whoa, what's wrong?" My homeroom friend Maya is inside, washing her hands, wearing the Janet Jackson *Rhythm Nation 1814* T-shirt I'm so envious of. I rush over to her.

"Maya. Oh my God. Dave grabbed me."

"Finally."

"No"—my voice is grave, and Maya looks confused— "I mean, he grabbed me the bad way. He sexually assaulted me."

Maya laughs. "What?"

"He slid his hand up and grabbed my vagina, in the dark, to old British men on TV doing improv!"

Her face changes as she tosses her paper towel into the trash. The confusion is replaced with a sneer. It is clear that Maya thinks I am the biggest moron on the planet.

"That means he likes you, you idiot."

I hold my breath while watching Janet's tour dates leave the room and then turn and look at myself in the mirror. My mouth is open. I close it, pull my Kissing Kooler lip gloss out of my pocket, and mash the watermelon flavor onto my lips. I am so mad that Dave ruined this crush; I didn't want him to touch me, especially on the vagina. He is a terrible person and so is Maya. I am thirteen years old.

I GO BACK TO Twitter and read as the stories and tweets and retweets come in even faster than a few minutes ago, when I asked women to share. Thousands. I feel myself slipping into that quiet place, but I fight the urge, realizing this is bigger than myself. My white-hot rage has opened up a global platform for women on Twitter, people are paying attention. I add a hashtag to my tweets.

Women: keep tweeting me assaults with #notokay

Here was my second assault:

Boy in drama class grabbed my "pussy" during class, I was 13.

WINTER 1992

"Betty Ann said he's weird. I am not sure. I think he's a bit off, though, and not easy to talk to." My mom is whispering this to me into the ear I've pulled The Sundays' version of "Wild Horses" away from.

"And?"

"Just, do you want me to come in with you?"

"To my dermatologist appointment for my acne? Mom. No."

I'm fine. I pull my headphone back over my ear. I've been listening to a lot of music lately. I have come to the realization that I'm a *very* emotional person, and song lyrics make me feel a lot of feelings. I enjoy feeling these feelings. The words in the songs are much more interesting and relevant to me than the words I normally listen to, such as Mom's words.

I wait, in a gown, in the chair for patients in his office.

When I was younger, I was so proud of my acne. I'd show it off to everyone I knew and even those I didn't. "These aren't chicken pox, they are *zits*!" I was in sixth grade and I'd skip around the park alone like a happy schizophrenic yelling and singing to myself about my acne and how grown up I was.

But now, I'm actually a teenager and pus on my face is making me look too messy, too oily, too . . .

"Kelly, I'm Dr. _____. I see you're here for acne?"

I point to my face, then make a face, opening my eyes wide.

"I think I got a problem, Doc!"

"Yes, let me see." He looks at my face briefly and then opens my file.

"Allergic to anything?"

"Dogs. Mostly just retrievers and shepherds."

"I meant medications."

"Oh, not that I know of, I haven't taken many. There are a lot of medicines out there."

He passes me a prescription. He is immune to my amazing teenage sarcasm.

"I see you have a lot of moles."

"I probably have as many moles as there are medicines, this is true." He laughs, I laugh. Score. Why did Betty Ann think this guy was weird?

"Can you take off that robe for me?"

"Sorry?"

What did he just say?

"I'd like to check your moles." Oh, right.

"Oh, right."

I untie the string at the back of my neck and pull the gown forward, scrunching it down to my waist. He looks at my arms.

"Can you stand up, please?"

"Sure." I stand, in a bra, with my headphones around my neck, holding my gown at my waist.

I assure him, as he looks at my sides, "None of them are sore or irregular or black or bleeding. I know the rules, I'm basically a hypochondriac."

"Remove your bra."

Involuntarily I laugh. "I don't have any moles on my boobs."

"Come in here." He walks toward the entry to his office and I follow. He touches my shoulder and guides me to stand me the middle of the small room, blocking the doorway with his body. He looks at me.

"We'll just check your breasts and then we're all done."

I take off my bra. He stares intently and then touches my mole-less boobs. I look down and see his hand sweep one, and then the other.

"Great. Get dressed and we can book a follow-up for your acne." He leaves. The door closes.

I quickly tug my bra into place, snapping it back on, grab my shit and headphones, and play "Wild Horses." I need to hear "Wild Horses."

"Do you have everything, dear?" I'm greeted by a cheerful nurse as I walk out of the examination room.

"Yes," I think I say, but I can't hear myself as I have the music turned so loud. That music is my new silent lake.

I walk into the waiting room and my mom looks up. She says something I can't hear. I point to my headphones, then hold up the prescription. Mom takes it. I was fifteen years old.

MY HASHTAG #NOTOKAY IS flashing into my feed over and over again. I check to see what these women are tweeting at me. I can't be the only one reading these at this point. I want everyone to read them. And simultaneously, I want them to disappear. It is awful. It is real.

- *At 7, in grocery store, man presses his penis on my neck. This is my second tweet ever. #notokay*
- *Guy interviewing me for a job tries to get my clothes off, I'm 15. #notokay*
- *#notokay in 1941 my bible teacher, my dad's best friend molested me and my sister. Ages 13 & 7. Some things don't change.*
- *Chiropractor rests his clothed genitals on my hand. Scared. No one was around #notokay*
- *40yo guitar teacher teaches me to strum by stroking my leg. He asks to kiss me. I'm 13 and I don't go back #notokay*
- *He was a friend giving me a ride home. I just wanted to get away. #notokay*
- *I can't send mine without losing my peace. Thank you for doing this. #notokay*
- *My brother raped me repeatedly for 3 years, told me it was my fault I was born a girl. I was 9. #notokay*
- *Age 7, guy masturbates while watching me play handball. Mom calls cops. I can't remember color of pants. He goes free.*
- *First time I remember I was 7. Mom's BFF. Pretty sure he was the first. Not the last. #notokay*
- *I don't remember the first time. I just know my mom took me from bio-dad at 8 months after catching him. #notokay*
- *I made anon acct to reply: I was maybe 8, my older cousin put his hand down my pants and underwear and in me.*

KELLY OXFORD

- *High school civics teacher would rub the feet of an attractive student in the front row. She had no choice. #notokay*
- *Man on street walks by, moans in my ear "The things I'd do to you."*
- *Dad didn't believe me. #notokay*
- *Pediatrician neighbor teaches me how to masturbate, tries to get me to do it beside him. I'm 12.*
- *Podiatrist grazes my breasts while examining my foot. Felt violated. Kept quiet.*
- *Just one assault? A pelvic exam in ER. My back was hurt from gymnastics class.*
- *At my gram's funeral my 90 year old uncle says he wants to fuck me. His wife laughs it off. #notokay*

I see that my Twitter account is trending in Los Angeles, Seattle, Chicago, New York. But that simply means that enough people are replying to me that my name is trending. These tweets could still go totally unknown. I have to make sure other people see this. I owe it to everyone who has responded to me. So, I decide to tweet: *1 hr ago I shared my sexual assault & asked if you could do the same. Look at my timeline. 1000s of stories. We must discuss. Not our shame. #notokay*

This will draw the press in, I think, telling people it's here is all I can do now.

WINTER 1994

He plays Hole's album whenever I want.

"Trevor? One more time."

"That was twice."

Trevor plays that record whenever I want, unless it's just been played twice in a row.

"I'm going to get a *K* tattoo between my boobs, just like Courtney Love."

"That's . . . original."

I laugh. "But it will be on me and there is only one me so you're right. It is original! Get me another slime, Trevor!"

Trevor has long hair like Eddie Vedder but is better looking than Eddie Vedder. He has a fiancée named June, she is older than him and always tells me, "I used to be just like you." Which makes me hopeful that one day I will have a boyfriend who is hotter than Eddie Vedder.

Most important, Trevor lets me and my friends Karen and Erin into the bar even though we are underage.

If I could live at this bar I would. From Friday night to Sunday I spend sixteen-plus hours here drinking and then throwing up. At the end of all of that I go home and watch *60 Minutes* with my parents.

I'm not old enough to vote but I spend every weekend completely drunk.

Trevor passes me a pint glass full of electric-green lime juice and vodka, aka slime, and I look out the windows.

"Trevor, I love you."

"I love you, too."

"No, I mean it." Neither of us actually means it.

Earlier this year I broke up with my high school boy-friend of two years.

Alex and I were very much *in love,* like only codependent children can be. Alex is the one who first brought me to this bar, his fake ID denied. My fake ID, made exactly the same way, was accepted.

I watched Alex and our other male high school friends get asked to leave. Banned, in fact. They were older than I was. I stayed because I was selfish and I got into the bar. This was a personal coup against "the man," not him.

However, now? Coming to this bar every weekend and hanging out with university guys is payback to Alex for fuck-ing my friends after our breakup. Part of my justification for getting drunk all the time now is that I'd lost all of my friends to him after our breakup. He was part of a group of grungy cute boys, he was clearly into commitment; I mean, after two years of being a loyal boyfriend to me, what teen girl wouldn't want to be with that? I'm sure he told all of them that I broke up with him because I didn't want to marry him. Not that he'd asked, but we'd been together for two years and I was ready to meet other guys I could pos-sibly become infatuated with. We were only seventeen, for Christ's sake.

I am drunk, dancing alone to The Offspring in this bar that hangs over the city.

"Want some of this?" A guy holds a weirdly small joint out for me.

"Hell, yes!" I puff a little, then a little more. I taste metal.

"Hey, your shit tastes gross, dude." Shaking my head in disgust, I pass the joint back to him.

"Oh! Sorry. That's my fault."

"What is your fault?"

"Joint. It's a coco puff. Cocaine. Should have warned you."

"You dick! Trevor!"

Maybe cocaine makes me less cool because I promptly run back to the bar to tattle on the guy who just let me smoke cocaine. I'm not above rule breaking but I didn't want any other girls to be laced by some seemingly innocuous stoner's coco puff.

"Trevor, that guy is smoking a joint in here." Trevor cups his hands over his mouth. "JOINTS OUTSIDE!"

"Trevor, did you know the only guy I like right now has a girlfriend and she threatened to stab me?"

"Yes. I did know that."

I've explained this to Trevor a million times.

"Did you know that I love Oprah like a mother?"

"Yes."

That, too.

I look down the hall to my girlfriends Karen and Erin, sitting with a few guys from the university hockey team. I decide to join them. Karen is one of my closest friends but I think she secretly hates me. This is because once she was hooking up with this awful athlete, and I knew he was a creep. So, I kept going into the room while they were trying to fuck. I turned on the light. I so unsexually got into bed with them and started talking about the weather. I told her she should leave. I was thrown out repeatedly because I was being a huge asshole, but I kept going back in, drunk, but determined to save her vagina. I remember her telling me something along the lines of "You're just jealous."

And that was partly true, I mean, I wished I could just have sex for the sake of horniness . . . but I was not there. I needed something more. I needed someone to genuinely like me for me. As a teenage girl with a body that society has deemed attractive, it's very clear you can get a large percentage of guys to have sex with you. That really didn't turn me on.

But tonight, all seems right in the world and between Karen, Erin, and me. I lean over to Erin.

"Hey! I love you."

"I love you," Erin says in her deep voice, pulling me in for a hug before kissing my cheek. Erin and I both have Ukrainian grandparents and we do love each other. She and Karen may be closer, but Erin and I have a dark streak we share. We talk about people on a psychological level with each other. Erin is my first friend of this nature, and I cherish her.

"Erin, I don't think I've peed all night." At the table are the hockey players Jesse, Dylan, Tim, Ross, and Warren. All are regulars, except for Warren. I'd never hung out with Warren. We were friendly with these guys and would flirt back and forth with consent, harmlessly.

"Pee, girl, pee!"

I dance to "99 Luftballons" all the way down the hall to

the bathroom, as only a drunk person can. Carefree, cinematically, as if my life is perfect.

I push into a dirty stall and take one of the longest pees of my life. The kind where you think it's over and then suddenly realize there's possibly a second bladder tucked up behind the first one. This is another thing that only seems to happen to drunk people.

"The seal has broken," I whisper to myself in an overly dramatic, silly way, "and now you will be in this dirty stall all night. You'll be here every five minutes."

I pull the stall door in and gasp. Warren is standing in the bathroom, facing me. He is six foot five and probably the best-looking human being in this bar. His face is Denzel Washington symmetrical. He looks angry. I open my mouth but I don't know what to say. My fight-or-flight instinct is raging but I'm frozen, unable to react. I know that this situation will not end well, and my mind begins to go to that dark place when he grabs my waist and picks me up. I feel like I'm a child, not sure why an adult is picking me up. Adults don't announce their actions to children, they just do them. What is happening? Are we about to re-create the Johnny and Baby performance from *Dirty Dancing*?

"Why are you in the girls' bathroom?" I ask mid-air before he lowers me into a wet sink and spreads my legs with his body. His perfect mouth comes close to my face, seething with hate. He is so close, I can feel his sweat and his spit as he begins to speak. "Do you know what rape is?" he hisses into my mouth, grabbing my body. My mind goes blank. A moment later Dylan enters the bathroom.

"DUDE." Though significantly smaller, he grabs Warren's shoulder. Warren puts his tongue in my mouth, then spits on me. Dylan leads him out of the bathroom, but Warren turns and looks back at me, eyes full of rage.

I'm left in a sink. Tasting Warren's Jack and Coke, feeling the damp of people's dirty hands seep through the bottom of my pants. I hop out of the sink, and walk back into the bar to "Tainted Love." Warren and Dylan are nowhere to be seen.

I walk right to Erin and sit on her lap, suddenly sober.

"Eew, you're wet."

"Warren came in the bathroom and asked me if I knew what rape was. He put his tongue in my mouth and then spit on me. Dylan saved me."

Erin's eyes widen, hand to her heart. We would protect each other from this day forward. I was seventeen years old.

WHEN I WAS TWELVE and the old man grabbed my vagina on the bus, I felt shame, because I was truly trying to get the attention of a boy and I innately felt as though putting hair spray in my hair had invited the grabbing. When the boy whose attention I so desperately wanted finally gave it to me, in Drama class, my friend made me feel like I should be grateful. I was so confused that a doctor would do anything so wrong, that I said nothing, because clearly it had to be me who had done something wrong. And Warren, well, he was just teaching me a lesson, right? I probably shouldn't drink so much and I definitely shouldn't go to the bathroom alone. Girls who do that could get raped.

I've always felt like rape is the invisible vampire I had to run from, if vampires were real and everywhere, all the time. Because I've never been raped, I've always waited for it, wondering where and when. Dark parking lots, elevators, bathrooms, hotel rooms, my front yard, my own bed. I feel it could happen. Anytime. All the time. I'm ready to fight, but I'm almost forty. I'm fucking tired, you guys.

I feel lucky that I've only have a handful of experiences with sexual assault. Of my five closest friends all of us have been assaulted, none of us has been raped. But among our mothers, sisters, friends, there are many who have— on dates, by family members, in the street. This is fucked. And now, a man running to be the President of the United States is making jokes about it. Making jokes about how he can do anything to a woman, he can grab them in the pussy.

Now more than 3 million women have been to my Twitter page and shared stories of strangers, relatives, family friends, close friends, peers, doctors, teachers, police officers, touching them. *More than 3 million.* The media have picked up on this: *Vogue, Washington Post, Huffington Post, Boston Globe,* everyone is talking about Trump, but everyone is also talking about the unraveling of secrets that I helped create this afternoon. My head is spinning. By the end of this week, more than 40 million people will read my tweets and share stories. I'll have been on the cover of the *New York Times* and on TV panels with Professor Anita Hill.

What is the story of women in this country? The neurotic witch hunts, being treated as property. Being kept in the home to raise children and make our men's lives easier. Being denied access to jobs we deserve or the recognition and equal pay for jobs we've done.

In the last one hundred years we've won the right to vote.

We've become leaders in politics, in industry, in media, in the arts.

Why haven't men stopped talking about us and touching us as though we are their objects? When will it ever stop?

Gertie jumps on the bed. I hold my hand out to pet her. We approach this moment as equals.

I turn off the television. I have to let the world go for now.

I don't know when this will all stop. Or when women will truly be equals. Sometimes I feel so alone, and other times I open my mouth or reach out and find that everyone is feeling the same way that I'm feeling. And that the world wants to discuss those feelings, no matter how painful. The sharing is maybe the thing that helps us see that the world isn't really against us after all.

Maybe.

CLOSING REMARKS

This book, and my first book, contain accurate depictions of the stories I've told myself in order to survive. I hope yours are twice as funny.

—Sincerely,
Kelly Oxford

ACKNOWLEDGMENTS

I won't be able to adequately express how much the positivity of my editors, Carrie Thornton and Kate Cassaday, helped me move through the days I worked on this book. Thank you for dealing with me when I was a 2.5 out of 10.

To Erin Malone, who made it all happen after I handed her my book proposal. Without you, there would be no this. Thank you.

Thank you to my kids, Sal, Henry, and Bea, and to their father, James, for being my inspiration to create and get out of bed.

I am grateful to my parents and sister for being who they are and staying on my team.

ACKNOWLEDGMENTS

Thank you to the following people for supporting me as I wrote these stories, by checking in and caring so much: Angela Brown, Alex McAtee, Kimberly Muller, Chloe Gosselin, Joseph Papa, Orlando Soria, Molly McNearney, Johnny Rice, Laura Brown, Constance Zimmer, Dawn O'Porter, Jacqui Getty, and David Jackson.

And to the Beverly Wilshire and Hotel Covell for being the places I most love to write.

ABOUT THE AUTHOR

Kelly Oxford, born in Edmonton, Canada, currently lives in Los Angeles with her three children. She likes poodles and PBS.